Elementary World History—You Report!

MASTER BOOKS
—CURRICULUM—

Authors: Tim Lovett, Bodie Hodge, Randy & Kristen Pratt

Master Books Creative Team:

Editor: Craig Froman

Design: Jennifer Bauer

Cover Design: Diana Bogardus

Copy Editors:
Judy Lewis

Willow Meek

Curriculum Review:
Kristen Pratt
Laura Welch
Diana Bogardus

First printing: June 2017
Fourth printing: September 2019

Master Books®, P.O. Box 726, Green Forest, AR 72638

Master Books® is a division of the New Leaf Publishing Group, Inc.

ISBN: 978-1-68344-099-4
ISBN: 978-1-61458-609-8 (digital)

Printed in the United States of America

Please visit our website for other great titles:
www.masterbooks.com

Affordable
Flexible
Faith Building

MASTER BOOKS
—CURRICULUM—

Table of Contents

Author Bios:

Tim Lovett (*Noah's Ark: Thinking Outside the Box* book) did extensive research into wooden ships and modern maritime lore to understand the marvellous design of Noah's ark and its ability to survive the cataclysmic Flood.

Bodie Hodge (*Big Book of History*) attended Southern Illinois University at Carbondale and received a B.S. and M.S. in mechanical engineering. Currently, Bodie is a speaker, writer, and researcher for Answers in Genesis–USA. He is the author of *The Fall of Satan* and co-author of *Dragons: Legends & Lore of Dinosaurs*.

Randy Pratt and his wonderful wife Kristen have 9 children, successfully graduating 5, and 4 still actively homeschooling. Randy has served as a principal of a Christian school, developed a homeschool curriculum distribution business, pastored a growing church, and is now serving as vice president of sales & marketing at Master Books with a passion to serve the homeschool community.

Features: The suggested weekly schedule enclosed has easy-to-manage lessons that guide the reading, worksheets, and all assessments. The pages of this guide are perforated and three-hole punched so materials are easy to tear out, hand out, grade, and store. Teachers are encouraged to adjust the schedule and materials needed in order to best work within their unique educational program.

Lesson Scheduling: Students are instructed to read the pages in their book and then complete the corresponding section provided by the teacher. Assessments that may include worksheets, activities, quizzes, and tests are given at regular intervals with space to record each grade. Space is provided on the weekly schedule for assignment dates, and flexibility in scheduling is encouraged. Teachers may adapt the scheduled days per each unique student situation. As the student completes each assignment, this can be marked with an "X" in the box.

🕐	Approximately 30 to 45 minutes per lesson, three days a week
🔑	Includes answer keys for 88 assignment worksheets
📝	Assignment for each panel of *Big Book of History*
🔁	Built-in activities teach research and essay writing
📄	Designed for grades 4 to 6 in a one-year history course

Course Description

This *Elementary World History—You Report!* contains materials for use with *Big Book of History* and *Noah's Ark: Thinking Outside the Box.* Students will look at the individual panels of the *Big Book of History* and then complete the appropriate assignment worksheets in the teacher guide. They should be encouraged to complete as many of them as possible, as well as working on those related to the research paper in order to develop these important skills. The goal is to help students develop an understanding of different types of historical events and how they relate to others around the world in the same time period, while seeing clearly how Christian history has always been part of the historical timeline of our world.

Student completing this course will learn about:

- ✔ Who the first emperors of China and Rome were
- ✔ What discovery unlocked the secrets of a forgotten language
- ✔ How modern robotics had its roots in the tea dolls of Japan
- ✔ Where Christians faced death for the entertainment of thousands
- ✔ Why the languages of Greek and Hebrew were used to write the Bible
- ✔ How an ancient ship could be constructed that would survive the global Flood

You Report! is a fun way to learn about world history from Creation to present day. Using the *Big Book of History* timeline, your student will be the reporter, gathering information to report either orally or through writing.

You Report! is an overview of the history of the world. Through the use of role play, fun learning activities, and copy work, students will gain an understanding of the who, what, where, and when of history through a biblical, Christian worldview. **You Report!** sets a foundation to build upon. In future years, as your student begins to study the specifics of history, they will be able to put that information into the context of the greater picture.

To use **You Report!**, follow the lesson plan. The curriculum is designed to be done three days a week over 36 weeks. Two days a week are devoted to working through the *Big Book of History* timeline. The third day is spent working on a special assignment corresponding with the book *Noah's Ark: Thinking Outside the Box*. The curriculum is organized so that the sixth week in each section is a review of the material learned the previous five weeks.

Through the work done on assignments, building timelines, copy work, and reporting, students will have reviewed the information they have learned three to five times. If your student shows an interest in a particular person, event, or topic, you can supplement with additional materials and encourage them to learn more. The course is designed as an overview/introduction to history. It is not an exhaustive study of history but does provide the opportunity to go deeper if desired.

Grading Subjective Assignments

Most often grading is very objective. In math for example, 2 + 2 = 4, and no amount of individual expression changes this answer. However, there are times in this course when the answer may depend on a student's reflections of what he or she has learned on a particular day or in a week of assignments. In these subjective cases, the teacher can base a grade for these responses on several more objective measures. Does the student seem to understand the question and answer it as clearly as possible? Does the answer seem complete or does it fail to answer all aspects of the question? So a student may receive full credit if they seemed to meet all the assignment requirements, may get a passing grade if they meet some of the requirements, or may need to repeat the assignment if they didn't meet any of the requirements.

A – Student showed complete mastery of concepts with no errors.

B – Student showed mastery of concepts with minimal errors.

C – Student showed partial mastery of concepts. Review of some concepts is needed.

D – Student showed minimal understanding of concepts. Review is needed.

F – Student did not show understanding of concepts. Review is needed.

Students should make corrections on assignments but should be graded on the quality of their reports. Grades can be recorded as follows:

Week	Oral or Written Report	Grade
6	_____	_____
12	_____	_____
18	_____	_____
24	_____	_____
30	_____	_____
35	_____	_____
36	Special Written Report, Noah's Ark	_____
	Final Grade	_____

First Semester Suggested Daily Schedule

Date	Day	Assignment	Due Date	✓	Grade
		First Semester — First Quarter			
Week 1	Day 1	*Big Book of History* (BBOH) and *Elementary World History – You Report! Teacher Guide* (TG) **Assignment 1 — Time-lines** • Complete Worksheet Pages 19–20 (TG)			
	Day 2				
	Day 3	**Assignment 2 — In the Beginning** (BBOH) Complete Worksheet Pages 21–22 (TG)			
	Day 4				
	Day 5	**Assignment 3 — Special Report on Noah's Ark** *Noah's Ark: Thinking Outside the Box* (NA) Read Pages 8–11 (NA) • Complete Worksheet Page 23 (TG)			
Week 2	Day 6	**Assignment 4 — Adam Gets a Helper** (BBOH) Complete Worksheet Pages 25–26 (TG)			
	Day 7				
	Day 8	**Assignment 5 — Paradise Lost** (BBOH) Complete Worksheet Pages 27–28 (TG)			
	Day 9				
	Day 10	**Assignment 6 — Special Report on Noah's Ark** (NA) Read Pages 12–13 (NA) • Complete Worksheet Page 29 (TG)			
Week 3	Day 11	**Assignment 7 — We Need a Hero!** (BBOH) Complete Worksheet Page 31 (TG)			
	Day 12				
	Day 13	**Assignment 8 — Global Flooding Expected** (BBOH) Complete Worksheet Page 33 (TG)			
	Day 14				
	Day 15	**Assignment 9 — Special Report on Noah's Ark** (NA) Read Pages 14–15 (NA) • Complete Worksheet Page 35 (TG)			
Week 4	Day 16	**Assignment 10 — The Rainbow Is God's Sign** (BBOH) Complete Worksheet Pages 37–38 (TG)			
	Day 17				
	Day 18	**Assignment 11 — Major Ice Storm** (BBOH) Complete Worksheet Page 39 (TG)			
	Day 19				
	Day 20	**Assignment 12 — Special Report on Noah's Ark** (NA) Complete Worksheet Pages 41–42 (TG)			
Week 5	Day 21	**Assignment 13 — The Tower of Babel** (BBOH) Complete Worksheet Page 43 (TG)			
	Day 22				
	Day 23	**Assignment 14 — Flush Toilets** (BBOH) Complete Worksheet Page 45 (TG)			
	Day 24				
	Day 25	**Assignment 15 — Special Report on Noah's Ark** (NA) Read Pages 16–17 (NA) • Complete Worksheet Page 47 (TG)			

Date	Day	Assignment	Due Date	✓	Grade
	Day 26	**What We've Learned So Far** (BBOH) Complete Time-line Worksheet Pages 49–51 (TG)			
	Day 27				
Week 6	Day 28	**What We've Learned So Far** (BBOH) Complete Outline Worksheet Pages 53–54 (TG)			
	Day 29				
	Day 30	**What We've Learned So Far** (BBOH) Complete You Report! Worksheet Page 55 (TG)			
	Day 31	**Assignment 16 — Father Abraham** (BBOH) Complete Worksheet Page 57 (TG)			
	Day 32				
Week 7	Day 33	**Assignment 17 — Built with Rocks** (BBOH) Complete Worksheet Page 59 (TG)			
	Day 34				
	Day 35	**Assignment 18 — Special Report on Noah's Ark** (NA) Read Pages 18–19 (NA) • Complete Worksheet Page 61 (TG)			
	Day 36	**Assignment 19 — Remarkable Stories (Joseph)** (BBOH) Complete Worksheet Page 63 (TG)			
	Day 37				
Week 8	Day 38	**Assignment 20 — Genesis Comes to an End** (BBOH) Complete Worksheet Page 65 (TG)			
	Day 39				
	Day 40	**Assignment 21 — Special Report on Noah's Ark** (NA) Read Pages 20–21 (NA) • Complete Worksheet Page 67 (TG)			
	Day 41	**Assignment 22 — Frogs, Flies, & Death of Firstborns** (BBOH) Complete Worksheet Page 69 (TG)			
	Day 42				
Week 9	Day 43	**Assignment 23 — Learning to Be God's Nation** (BBOH) Complete Worksheet Page 71 (TG)			
	Day 44				
	Day 45	**Assignment 24 — Special Report on Noah's Ark** (NA) Read Pages 22–23 (NA) • Complete Worksheet Page 73 (TG)			

Date	Day	Assignment	Due Date	✓	Grade
		First Semester — Second Quarter			
Week 1	Day 46	**Assignment 25 — The Trojan Horse** (BBOH) Complete Worksheet Page 75 (TG)			
	Day 47				
	Day 48	**Assignment 26 — David vs. Goliath** (BBOH) Complete Worksheet Page 77 (TG)			
	Day 49				
	Day 50	**Assignment 27 — Special Report on Noah's Ark** (NA) Read Pages 24–25 (NA) • Complete Worksheet Page 79 (TG)			
Week 2	Day 51	**Assignment 28 — Dictionaries Used in China** (BBOH) Complete Worksheet Page 81 (TG)			
	Day 52				
	Day 53	**Assignment 29 — Solomon's Temple** (BBOH) Complete Worksheet Page 83 (TG)			
	Day 54				
	Day 55	**Assignment 30 — Special Report on Noah's Ark** (NA) Read Pages 26–27 (NA) • Complete Worksheet Page 85 (TG)			
Week 3	Day 56	**What We've Learned So Far** (BBOH) Complete Time-line Worksheet Pages 87–89 (TG)			
	Day 57				
	Day 58	**What We've Learned So Far** (BBOH) Complete Outline Worksheet Page 91 (TG)			
	Day 59				
	Day 60	**What We've Learned So Far** (BBOH) Complete You Report! Worksheet Page 93 (TG)			
Week 4	Day 61	**Assignment 31 — The First Olympics** (BBOH) Complete Worksheet Page 95 (TG)			
	Day 62				
	Day 63	**Assignment 32 — The Seven Wonders** (BBOH) Complete Worksheet Page 97 (TG)			
	Day 64				
	Day 65	**Assignment 33 — Special Report on Noah's Ark** (NA) Read Pages 28–29 (NA) • Complete Worksheet Page 99 (TG)			
Week 5	Day 66	**Assignment 34 — Daniel in Babylon** (BBOH) Complete Worksheet Page 101 (TG)			
	Day 67				
	Day 68	**Assignment 35 — Queen Esther Saves the Israelites** (BBOH) Complete Worksheet Page 103 (TG)			
	Day 69				
	Day 70	**Assignment 36 — Special Report on Noah's Ark** (NA) Complete Review Outline Page 105 (TG)			

Date	Day	Assignment	Due Date	✓	Grade
	Day 71	**Assignment 37 — Alexander the Great** (BBOH) Complete Worksheet Page 107 (TG)			
	Day 72				
Week 6	Day 73	**Assignment 38 — Roman Empire Conquers Greece** (BBOH) Complete Worksheet Page 109 (TG)			
	Day 74				
	Day 75	**Assignment 39 — Special Report on Noah's Ark** (NA) Read Pages 30–33 (NA) • Complete Worksheet Page 111 (TG)			
	Day 76	**Assignment 40 — The New Testament Begins** (BBOH) Complete Worksheet Page 113 (TG)			
	Day 77				
Week 7	Day 78	**Assignment 41 — The Difference Between B.C. and A.D.** (BBOH) Complete Worksheet Page 115 (TG)			
	Day 79				
	Day 80	**Assignment 42 — Special Report on Noah's Ark** (NA) Read Pages 34–35 (NA) • Complete Worksheet Page 117 (TG)			
	Day 81	**Assignment 43 — Our Hero Is Born!** (BBOH) Complete Worksheet Page 119 (TG)			
	Day 82				
Week 8	Day 83	**Assignment 44 — Jesus Is Risen!** (BBOH) Complete Worksheet Page 121 (TG)			
	Day 84				
	Day 85	**Assignment 45 — Special Report on Noah's Ark** (NA) Read Pages 36–37 (NA) • Complete Worksheet Page 123 (TG)			
	Day 86	**What We've Learned So Far** (BBOH) Complete Time-line Worksheet Pages 125–127 (TG)			
	Day 87				
Week 9	Day 88	**What We've Learned So Far** (BBOH) Complete Outline Worksheet Page 129 (TG)			
	Day 89				
	Day 90	**What We've Learned So Far** (BBOH) Complete You Report! Worksheet Page 131 (TG)			
		Midterm Grade			

Date	Day	Assignment	Due Date	✓	Grade
		Second Semester — Third Quarter			
Week 1	Day 91	**Assignment 46 — Hero of Alexandria** (BBOH) Complete Worksheet Page 133 (TG)			
	Day 92				
	Day 93	**Assignment 47 — Colossal Colosseum** (BBOH) Complete Worksheet Page 135 (TG)			
	Day 94				
	Day 95	**Assignment 48 — Special Report on Noah's Ark** (NA) Read Pages 38–39 (NA) • Complete Worksheet Page 137 (TG)			
Week 2	Day 96	**Assignment 49 — Death as a Sport** (BBOH) Complete Worksheet Page 139 (TG)			
	Day 97				
	Day 98	**Assignment 50 — You're Not My Mummy** (BBOH) Complete Worksheet Page 141 (TG)			
	Day 99				
	Day 100	**Assignment 51 — Special Report on Noah's Ark** (NA) Read Pages 40–41 (NA) • Complete Worksheet Page 143 (TG)			
Week 3	Day 101	**Assignment 52 — Brilliant Minds Still Make Mistakes!** (BBOH) Complete Worksheet Page 145 (TG)			
	Day 102				
	Day 103	**Assignment 53 — Roman Empire Split in Two** (BBOH) Complete Worksheet Page 147 (TG)			
	Day 104				
	Day 105	**Assignment 54 — Special Report on Noah's Ark** (NA) Read Pages 42–43 (NA) • Complete Worksheet Page 149 (TG)			
Week 4	Day 106	**Assignment 55 — The Edict of Milan** (BBOH) Complete Worksheet Page 151 (TG)			
	Day 107				
	Day 108	**Assignment 56 — Triumph of the Church** (BBOH) Complete Worksheet Page 153 (TG)			
	Day 109				
	Day 110	**Assignment 57 — Special Report on Noah's Ark** (NA) Read Pages 44–45 (NA) • Complete Worksheet Page 155 (TG)			
Week 5	Day 111	**Assignment 58 — The Bible is Translated into Latin** (BBOH) Complete Worksheet Page 157 (TG)			
	Day 112				
	Day 113	**Assignment 59 — The Birth of Islam** (BBOH) Complete Worksheet Page 159 (TG)			
	Day 114				
	Day 115	**Assignment 60 — Special Report on Noah's Ark** (NA) Read Pages 46–49 (NA) • Complete Worksheet Page 161 (TG)			

Date	Day	Assignment	Due Date	✓	Grade
	Day 116	**What We've Learned So Far** (BBOH) Complete Time-line Worksheet Pages 163–165 (TG)			
	Day 117				
Week 6	Day 118	**What We've Learned So Far** (BBOH) Complete Outline Worksheet Page 167 (TG)			
	Day 119				
	Day 120	**What We've Learned So Far** (BBOH) Complete You Report! Worksheet Page 169 (TG)			
	Day 121	**Assignment 61 — Genghis Khan** (BBOH) Complete Worksheet Page 171 (TG)			
	Day 122				
Week 7	Day 123	**Assignment 62 — The Bubonic Plague** (BBOH) Complete Worksheet Page 173 (TG)			
	Day 124				
	Day 125	**Assignment 63 — Special Report on Noah's Ark** (NA) Read Pages 50–51 (NA) • Complete Worksheet Page 175 (TG)			
	Day 126	**Assignment 64 — The Age of Discovery** (BBOH) Complete Worksheet Page 177 (TG)			
	Day 127				
Week 8	Day 128	**Assignment 65 — The Protestant Reformation** (BBOH) Complete Worksheet Page 179 (TG)			
	Day 129				
	Day 130	**Assignment 66 — Special Report on Noah's Ark** (NA) Read Pages 52–53 (NA) • Complete Worksheet Page 181 (TG)			
	Day 131	**Assignment 67 — "To Be or Not To Be" (Shakespeare)** (BBOH) Complete Worksheet Page 183 (TG)			
	Day 132				
Week 9	Day 133	**Assignment 68 — Pilgrims Reach Shore in America** (BBOH) Complete Worksheet Page 185 (TG)			
	Day 134				
	Day 135	**Assignment 69 — Special Report on Noah's Ark** (NA) Read Pages 54–55 (NA) • Complete Worksheet Page 187 (TG)			

Date	Day	Assignment	Due Date	✓	Grade
		Second Semester — Fourth Quarter			
Week 1	Day 136	**Assignment 70 — The Apple Doesn't Fall Far from the Tree (Newton)** (BBOH) Complete Worksheet Page 189 (TG)			
	Day 137				
	Day 138	**Assignment 71 — Father of Scientific Method (Galileo)** (BBOH) Complete Worksheet Page 191 (TG)			
	Day 139				
	Day 140	**Assignment 72 — Special Report on Noah's Ark** (NA) Complete Review Outline Page 193 (TG)			
Week 2	Day 141	**Assignment 73 — The Age of Reason** (BBOH) Complete Worksheet Page 195 (TG)			
	Day 142				
	Day 143	**Assignment 74 — The Industrial Revolution** (BBOH) Complete Worksheet Page 197 (TG)			
	Day 144				
	Day 145	**Assignment 75 — Special Report on Noah's Ark** (NA) Read Pages 56–59 (NA) • Complete Worksheet Page 199 (TG)			
Week 3	Day 146	**What We've Learned So Far** (BBOH) Complete Time-line Worksheet Pages 201–203 (TG)			
	Day 147				
	Day 148	**What We've Learned So Far** (BBOH) Complete Outline Worksheet Page 205 (TG)			
	Day 149				
	Day 150	**What We've Learned So Far** (BBOH) Complete You Report! Worksheet Page 207 (TG)			
Week 4	Day 151	**Assignment 76 — The Birth of a New Nation** (BBOH) Complete Worksheet Page 209 (TG)			
	Day 152				
	Day 153	**Assignment 77 — Ludwig van Beethoven** (BBOH) Complete Worksheet Page 211 (TG)			
	Day 154				
	Day 155	**Assignment 78 — Special Report on Noah's Ark** (NA) Read Pages 60–61 (NA) • Complete Worksheet Page 213 (TG)			
Week 5	Day 156	**Assignment 79 — Find the Dates** (BBOH) Complete Worksheet Page 215 (TG)			
	Day 157				
	Day 158	**Assignment 80 — Inventors of Fact and Fiction** (BBOH) Complete Worksheet Page 217 (TG)			
	Day 159				
	Day 160	**Assignment 81 — Special Report on Noah's Ark** (NA) Read Pages 62–63 (NA) • Complete Worksheet Page 219 (TG)			

Date	Day	Assignment	Due Date	✓	Grade
Week 6	Day 161	**Assignment 82 — Slavery Ends in the U.S.** (BBOH) Complete Worksheet Page 221 (TG)			
	Day 162				
	Day 163	**Assignment 83 — Find the Dates** (BBOH) Complete Worksheet Page 223 (TG)			
	Day 164				
	Day 165	**Assignment 84 — Special Report on Noah's Ark** (NA) Read Pages 66–67 (NA) • Complete Worksheet Page 225 (TG)			
Week 7	Day 166	**Assignment 85 — Man in Space** (BBOH) Complete Worksheet Page 227 (TG)			
	Day 167				
	Day 168	**Assignment 86 — The Nation Israel Reborn** (BBOH) Complete Worksheet Page 229 (TG)			
	Day 169				
	Day 170	**Assignment 87 — Special Report on Noah's Ark** (NA) Read Pages 68–71 (NA) • Complete Worksheet Page 231 (TG)			
Week 8	Day 171	**What We've Learned So Far** (BBOH) Complete Time-line Worksheet Pages 233–235 (TG)			
	Day 172				
	Day 173	**What We've Learned So Far** (BBOH) Complete Outline Worksheet Page 237 (TG)			
	Day 174				
	Day 175	**What We've Learned So Far** (BBOH) Complete You Report! Worksheet Page 239 (TG)			
Week 9	Day 176	**Assignment 88 — Special Report on Noah's Ark** (NA) Complete Outline Review Page 241 (TG)			
	Day 177				
	Day 178	**Special Report on Noah's Ark** (NA) Complete Rough Draft and Final Report Pages 243–245 (TG)			
	Day 179				
	Day 180	**Assignment 89 — What About You?** (BBOH) Complete Worksheet Page 247 (TG)			
		Semester Grade			

Worksheets

W🌐RLD TIMES

In the Beginning, God Created the Heavens and the Earth!

There is a Creator, and He has a plan for His creation

Our story begins where time itself begins — at the creation event as described by the Creator Himself in the book of Genesis.

The **Old Testament** book of Genesis is the first book of the Bible, and it means beginnings. In Genesis chapter 1, we read that God creates the heavens, the earth, and everything in them. While many men make guesses about when time began, only the Bible gives us an accurate eyewitness account.

The Genesis account of creation tells us that God created everything in six **literal** days and then rested on the seventh day. This is why we have a seven-day week, too.

The Bible also tells us that His creation was good. We can believe this because God is good, and He intended for His creation to be good as well.

When did it start getting not-so-good? Sorry to say, that's coming soon.

Using the Eyewitness Report, Attachment 2 on page 22 as an eyewitness account, **You Report!** the news and tell what God created on each day of that first week.

Words to Know

Literal — Means exactly as it says, not a story

Testament — Means an agreement

You Report! ✎

What did God create on day 1?

What did God create on day 2?

What did God create on day 3?

What did God create on day 4?

What did God create on day 5?

What did God create on day 6?

What did God do on day 7?

From: God the Creator

To: Mankind

Subject: The Way It All Began

Memo: This is the report as given to Moses by the Creator and reported in **Genesis 1**

Attachment: 2

EYEWITNESS REPORT

¹ In the beginning God created the heaven and the earth.

² And the earth was without form, and void; and darkness was upon the face of the deep. And the Spirit of God moved upon the face of the waters.

³ And God said, Let there be light: and there was light.

⁴ And God saw the light, that it was good: and God divided the light from the darkness.

⁵ And God called the light Day, and the darkness he called Night. And the evening and the morning were the first day.

⁶ And God said, Let there be a firmament in the midst of the waters, and let it divide the waters from the waters.

⁷ And God made the firmament, and divided the waters which were under the firmament from the waters which were above the firmament: and it was so.

⁸ And God called the firmament Heaven. And the evening and the morning were the second day.

⁹ And God said, Let the waters under the heaven be gathered together unto one place, and let the dry land appear: and it was so.

¹⁰ And God called the dry land Earth; and the gathering together of the waters called he Seas: and God saw that it was good.

¹¹ And God said, Let the earth bring forth grass, the herb yielding seed, and the fruit tree yielding fruit after his kind, whose seed is in itself, upon the earth: and it was so.

¹² And the earth brought forth grass, and herb yielding seed after his kind, and the tree yielding fruit, whose seed was in itself, after his kind: and God saw that it was good.

¹³ And the evening and the morning were the third day.

¹⁴ And God said, Let there be lights in the firmament of the heaven to divide the day from the night; and let them be for signs, and for seasons, and for days, and years:

¹⁵ And let them be for lights in the firmament of the heaven to give light upon the earth: and it was so.

¹⁶ And God made two great lights; the greater light to rule the day, and the lesser light to rule the night: he made the stars also.

¹⁷ And God set them in the firmament of the heaven to give light upon the earth,

¹⁸ And to rule over the day and over the night, and to divide the light from the darkness: and God saw that it was good.

¹⁹ And the evening and the morning were the fourth day.

²⁰ And God said, Let the waters bring forth abundantly the moving creature that hath life, and fowl that may fly above the earth in the open firmament of heaven.

²¹ And God created great whales, and every living creature that moveth, which the waters brought forth abundantly, after their kind, and every winged fowl after his kind: and God saw that it was good.

²² And God blessed them, saying, Be fruitful, and multiply, and fill the waters in the seas, and let fowl multiply in the earth.

²³ And the evening and the morning were the fifth day.

²⁴ And God said, Let the earth bring forth the living creature after his kind, cattle, and creeping thing, and beast of the earth after his kind: and it was so.

²⁵ And God made the beast of the earth after his kind, and cattle after their kind, and every thing that creepeth upon the earth after his kind: and God saw that it was good.

²⁶ And God said, Let us make man in our image, after our likeness: and let them have dominion over the fish of the sea, and over the fowl of the air, and over the cattle, and over all the earth, and over every creeping thing that creepeth upon the earth.

²⁷ So God created man in his own image, in the image of God created he him; male and female created he them.

²⁸ And God blessed them, and God said unto them, Be fruitful, and multiply, and replenish the earth, and subdue it: and have dominion over the fish of the sea, and over the fowl of the air, and over every living thing that moveth upon the earth.

²⁹ And God said, Behold, I have given you every herb bearing seed, which is upon the face of all the earth, and every tree, in the which is the fruit of a tree yielding seed; to you it shall be for meat.

³⁰ And to every beast of the earth, and to every fowl of the air, and to every thing that creepeth upon the earth, wherein there is life, I have given every green herb for meat: and it was so.

³¹ And God saw every thing that he had made, and, behold, it was very good. And the evening and the morning were the sixth day.

NOAH'S ARK:
THINKING OUTSIDE THE BOX

Every year the Pulitzer Prize is awarded to a journalist for distinguished writing in various categories. This year you are being given the opportunity to write your own Pulitzer Prize–worthy investigative report on Noah's ark. The basis of your research will be the *Noah's Ark: Thinking Outside the Box* book.

1. Turn to page 8 of your book and copy the Scripture (John 1:1) below.

_____

_____

_____

_____

_____

_____

_____

_____

_____

John 1:1

2. Now read pages 10 and 11 and fill in the blanks:

The Bible is the _____ of God. It has more than _____ authors spanning

over _____ years — yet it all fits together to point to the most influential person to ever

live: Christ of Nazareth. _____ of prophesies were actually fulfilled in His life, death, and

_____.

WORLD TIMES

ADAM GETS A HELPER

In the image of God, He created them

Adam and Eve

Words to Know

Nostrils — means nose

Cleave — means to adhere to, cling to, or join

More about Adam

✓ He was the first zoologist. He was the namer of the animals.

✓ The first farmer and landscaper placed in the garden to care for it

✓ The father of the human race

✓ Made in the image of God and the first human to have a relationship with God

✓ Adam lived to be 930 years old.

Using the Eyewitness Report found in Attachment 4 on page 26, fill in the blanks below.

On day 6 of creation, God created _____ in His own image . . . and the Lord God formed

man from the _____ of the ground, and breathed into his nostrils the breath of _____;

and man became a living soul. God put the man, Adam, into the garden of Eden to dress it and keep it.

And the Lord God said it is not good that man should be _____; I will make him a help meet

[a perfect helper] for him. And the Lord God caused a deep _____ to fall upon Adam, and

as he slept, God took one of Adam's ribs and made a _____, and brought her to Adam.

Then Adam said, this is _____ of my bones, and _____ of my flesh; she shall be called

_____ because she was taken out of Man. Therefore a man shall leave his father and

mother. And shall cleave unto his wife: and they shall be _____ flesh.

From: God the Creator

To: Mankind

Subject: The First Couple, Adam and Eve

Memo: This is the report as given to Moses by the Creator & reported in **Genesis 1 & 2**.

Attachment: 4

EYEWITNESS REPORT

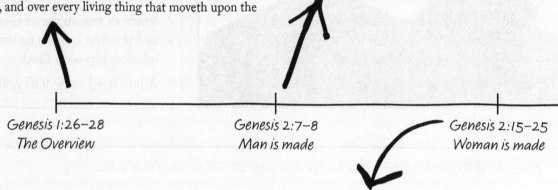

26 And God said, Let us make man in our image, after our likeness: and let them have dominion over the fish of the sea, and over the fowl of the air, and over the cattle, and over all the earth, and over every creeping thing that creepeth upon the earth.

27 So God created man in his own image, in the image of God created he him; male and female created he them.

28 And God blessed them, and God said unto them, Be fruitful, and multiply, and replenish the earth, and subdue it: and have dominion over the fish of the sea, and over the fowl of the air, and over every living thing that moveth upon the earth.

7 And the Lord God formed man of the dust of the ground, and breathed into his nostrils the breath of life; and man became a living soul.

8 And the Lord God planted a garden eastward in Eden; and there he put the man whom he had formed.

Genesis 1:26–28
The Overview

Genesis 2:7–8
Man is made

Genesis 2:15–25
Woman is made

15 And the Lord God took the man, and put him into the garden of Eden to dress it and to keep it.

16 And the Lord God commanded the man, saying, Of every tree of the garden thou mayest freely eat:

17 But of the tree of the knowledge of good and evil, thou shalt not eat of it: for in the day that thou eatest thereof thou shalt surely die.

18 And the Lord God said, It is not good that the man should be alone; I will make him an help meet for him.

19 And out of the ground the Lord God formed every beast of the field, and every fowl of the air; and brought them unto Adam to see what he would call them: and whatsoever Adam called every living creature, that was the name thereof.

20 And Adam gave names to all cattle, and to the fowl of the air, and to every beast of the field; but for Adam there was not found an help meet for him.

21 And the Lord God caused a deep sleep to fall upon Adam, and he slept: and he took one of his ribs, and closed up the flesh instead thereof;

22 And the rib, which the Lord God had taken from man, made he a woman, and brought her unto the man.

23 And Adam said, This is now bone of my bones, and flesh of my flesh: she shall be called Woman, because she was taken out of Man.

24 Therefore shall a man leave his father and his mother, and shall cleave unto his wife: and they shall be one flesh.

25 And they were both naked, the man and his wife, and were not ashamed.

WORLD TIMES

PARADISE LOST

Adam and Eve Are Banished from Eden

Today you are an investigative reporter. It is your assignment to read Attachment 4 to learn more about how paradise was lost, then draw a line from each of the four events to where each event occurred on the time-line below. You will need to draw a picture of the evidence in the blank as found on Attachment 5 on page 28.

The Tree with Forbidden Fruit

②

Flaming Sword

①

The Paradise Lost Timeline

Crafty Serpent

③

The Evidence (Draw the Picture)

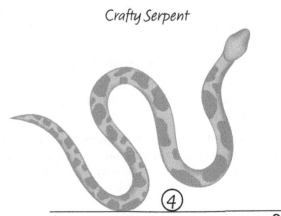

④

From: God the Creator

To: Mankind

Subject: The Man and Woman Sin

Memo: This is the report as given to Moses by the Creator and reported in **Genesis 3**

¹ Now the serpent was more subtil than any beast of the field which the Lord God had made. And he said unto the woman, Yea, hath God said, Ye shall not eat of every tree of the garden?

² And the woman said unto the serpent, We may eat of the fruit of the trees of the garden:

³ But of the fruit of the tree which is in the midst of the garden, God hath said, Ye shall not eat of it, neither shall ye touch it, lest ye die.

⁴ And the serpent said unto the woman, Ye shall not surely die:

⁵ For God doth know that in the day ye eat thereof, then your eyes shall be opened, and ye shall be as gods, knowing good and evil.

⁶ And when the woman saw that the tree was good for food, and that it was pleasant to the eyes, and a tree to be desired to make one wise, she took of the fruit thereof, and did eat, and gave also unto her husband with her; and he did eat.

⁷ And the eyes of them both were opened, and they knew that they were naked; and they sewed fig leaves together, and made themselves aprons.

⁸ And they heard the voice of the Lord God walking in the garden in the cool of the day: and Adam and his wife hid themselves from the presence of the Lord God amongst the trees of the garden.

⁹ And the Lord God called unto Adam, and said unto him, Where art thou?

¹⁰ And he said, I heard thy voice in the garden, and I was afraid, because I was naked; and I hid myself.

¹¹ And he said, Who told thee that thou wast naked? Hast thou eaten of the tree, whereof I commanded thee that thou shouldest not eat?

¹² And the man said, The woman whom thou gavest to be with me, she gave me of the tree, and I did eat.

¹³ And the Lord God said unto the woman, What is this that thou hast done? And the woman said, The serpent beguiled me, and I did eat.

¹⁴ And the Lord God said unto the serpent, Because thou hast done this, thou art cursed above all cattle, and above every beast of the field; upon thy belly shalt thou go, and dust shalt thou eat all the days of thy life:

¹⁵ And I will put enmity between thee and the woman, and between thy seed and her seed; it shall bruise thy head, and thou shalt bruise his heel.

¹⁶ Unto the woman he said, I will greatly multiply thy sorrow and thy conception; in sorrow thou shalt bring forth children; and thy desire shall be to thy husband, and he shall rule over thee.

¹⁷ And unto Adam he said, Because thou hast hearkened unto the voice of thy wife, and hast eaten of the tree, of which I commanded thee, saying, Thou shalt not eat of it: cursed is the ground for thy sake; in sorrow shalt thou eat of it all the days of thy life;

¹⁸ Thorns also and thistles shall it bring forth to thee; and thou shalt eat the herb of the field;

¹⁹ In the sweat of thy face shalt thou eat bread, till thou return unto the ground; for out of it wast thou taken: for dust thou art, and unto dust shalt thou return.

²⁰ And Adam called his wife's name Eve; because she was the mother of all living.

²¹ Unto Adam also and to his wife did the Lord God make coats of skins, and clothed them.

²² And the Lord God said, Behold, the man is become as one of us, to know good and evil: and now, lest he put forth his hand, and take also of the tree of life, and eat, and live for ever:

²³ Therefore the Lord God sent him forth from the garden of Eden, to till the ground from whence he was taken.

²⁴ So he drove out the man; and he placed at the east of the garden of Eden Cherubims, and a flaming sword which turned every way, to keep the way of the tree of life.

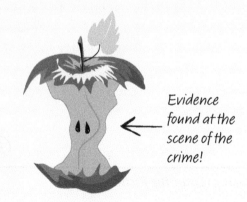

Evidence found at the scene of the crime!

NOAH'S ARK:
THINKING OUTSIDE THE BOX

Accepting God's Word as Truth

Our worldview is the set of beliefs we begin with as we look at the world around us. Every journalist has their own view of the stories they report based on their experiences and worldview. As you begin working on this special report of Noah's ark, you need to ask yourself a very basic question about your worldview.

1. Do you believe the Bible is true and can be trusted as a reliable source? (Circle One).

    YES   NO

If you answered yes, then you are starting with a biblical worldview, and the world simply makes more sense when we believe the God of creation. The biblical account of Noah's ark and the Flood helps us better understand the world we live in.

2. Read pages 12–13 in *Noah's Ark: Thinking Outside the Box*.

3. Copy the Scripture found on page 12 (Genesis 6:16–18) below.

_____

_____

_____

_____

_____

_____

_____

_____

_____

_____

Genesis 6:16–18

W🌐RLD TIMES

WE NEED A HERO!

All of history tells God's story. From the creation to today, we see God as an active participant in this story. In our last assignment we learned that because of the disobedience of Adam and Eve, they and their **descendants** were cursed. This event is also known as "the Fall."

Since we are all descendants of Adam and Eve, we also are subject to the Curse and in need of a hero to save us. We are all affected by "the Fall." We see it in struggle, death, and even thorns.

But in Genesis 3:15, God gives us a hint of a coming hero, a descendant of Eve who will bruise the head of the serpent and restore the relationship between God and man.

Sometimes a reporter needs to investigate a little further. Through Scripture, we can find that Jesus is a descendant of Eve.

Look at 1 Corinthians 15:22 found below. Who do you think our coming hero is going to be?

_____

Genesis 3:14-15

14 And the Lord God said unto the serpent, Because thou hast done this, thou art cursed above all cattle, and above every beast of the field; upon thy belly shalt thou go, and dust shalt thou eat all the days of thy life:

15 And I will put enmity between thee and the woman, and between thy seed and her seed; it shall bruise thy head, and thou shalt bruise his heel.

Words to Know
Descendants — Those related to
Investigate — To look into further
Serpent — Is later identified as Satan, the great enemy of God's people.
Enmity — Deep-seated, mutual hatred
Seed — Descendant of

Copy this verse on the line below.

"For as in Adam all die, even so in Christ (Jesus) shall all be made alive."

1 Corinthians 15:22

_____

_____

_____

_____

1 Corinthians 15:22

WRLD TIMES

GLOBAL FLOODING EXPECTED

1. From time-line on panel 2 of the *Big Book of History*, fill in the year of the Flood above.

Find your Bible and read chapter 7 in Genesis. Genesis is the first book in the Bible. Then answer the following questions:

2. How many days and nights did it rain?

_____

3. How many of the earth's high hills were covered?

_____

4. How many cubits upward did the water prevail?

_____

5. How many days did the waters prevail upon the earth?

_____

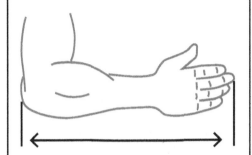

What Is a Cubit?

A cubit is measured from the end of the elbow to the end of the fingertips. Because everyone's cubit is different, we have to estimate how long Noah's cubit was. It is estimated that Noah's cubit was about 20 inches long.

6. Based on Genesis 7, "You Report!" and write a special weather report below.

You Report! ✏

NOAH'S ARK:
THINKING OUTSIDE THE BOX

Destruction

1. Read pages 14–15 in *Noah's Ark: Thinking Outside the Box.*

2. Fill in the blanks below:

Without _____ and without a true

knowledge and understanding of _____,

which provides the _____ history, man

is doomed to repeat the same _____

over and over.

3. Copy the following Scripture below.

"...All the fountains of the great deep broken up, and the windows of heaven were opened."

_____

_____

_____

_____

_____

_____

_____

_____

_____

_____

Genesis 7:11

GENESIS 7:11

W🌐RLD TIMES

THE RAINBOW IS GOD'S SIGN

Read about the agreement God made with Noah found in Attachment 10 on page 38 and answer the following questions:

1. What did God promise to never do again?

_____

_____

_____

2. What was the token of His agreement?

_____

_____

_____

3. Color in the rainbow below.

Words to Know
Bow — A rainbow
Covenant — An agreement
Spake — Spoke
Token — Something representing something

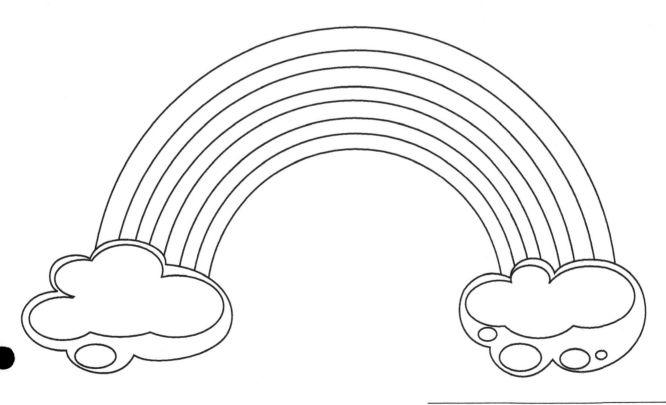

From: God the Creator

To: Mankind

Subject: The agreement God made with Noah and all flesh

Memo: This is the agreement given to Noah by the Creator and reported in **Genesis 9**

Attachment: 10

THE AGREEMENT

[8] And God spake unto Noah, and to his sons with him, saying,

[9] And I, behold, I establish my covenant with you, and with your seed after you;

[10] And with every living creature that is with you, of the fowl, of the cattle, and of every beast of the earth with you; from all that go out of the ark, to every beast of the earth.

[11] And I will establish my covenant with you, neither shall all flesh be cut off any more by the waters of a flood; neither shall there any more be a flood to destroy the earth.

[12] And God said, This is the token of the covenant which I make between me and you and every living creature that is with you, for perpetual generations:

[13] I do set my bow in the cloud, and it shall be for a token of a covenant between me and the earth.

[14] And it shall come to pass, when I bring a cloud over the earth, that the bow shall be seen in the cloud:

[15] And I will remember my covenant, which is between me and you and every living creature of all flesh; and the waters shall no more become a flood to destroy all flesh.

[16] And the bow shall be in the cloud; and I will look upon it, that I may remember the everlasting covenant between God and every living creature of all flesh that is upon the earth.

[17] And God said unto Noah, This is the token of the covenant, which I have established between me and all flesh that is upon the earth.

W🌐RLD TIMES

MAJOR ICE STORM

One-Third of the World Covered in Ice

Look at panel 2 of the *Big Book of History*. Can you find what caused the Ice Age?
Copy the "Did You Know?" section on the Ice Age below.

_____

_____

_____

_____

_____

_____

_____

_____

_____

_____

_____

_____

_____

_____

NOAH'S ARK:
THINKING OUTSIDE THE BOX

We have finished Section 1 of *Noah's Ark: Thinking Outside the Box*. Time-lines are one way we can organize information. Another is to create an outline of the information. Copy the following outline of what we've learned on the following page.

I.   What I've learned in Section 1 about the Word of God and the Biblical directive.

        A. The Word is the Bible.

        B. There were over 40 authors over thousands of years.

        C. All of the Bible points to Jesus.

II.   We need to accept God's Word as truth regarding the Flood and Noah's ark

III.   God promised to send a flood as judgment but spared Noah and his family.

Be sure to save this outline to use with your final project.

I.   What I've learned in Section 1 about the Word of God and the Biblical directive.

    A. _____

    _____

    B. _____

    _____

    C. _____

    _____

II.   _____

    _____

III.   _____

    _____

Be sure to save this outline to use with your final project.

W🌐RLD TIMES

THE TOWER OF BABEL

The First Recorded Skyscraper Is Built

1. From the time-line on panel 2 of the *Big Book of History*, fill in the year of the Tower of Babel above.

Find your Bible and read chapter 11 verses 1–9 in Genesis. Then answer the following questions:

2. How many languages did everyone speak?

_____

3. How high was the tower?

_____

4. What did God do to their language?

_____

5. What was the name of the city and the tower?

_____

6. Based on Genesis 11:1–9, "You Report!" and write a short news summary titled "Everyone Is Babel-ing."

You Report! ✏

THE TOWER OF BABEL

The First Recorded Skyscraper Is Built

Your Help Is Needed!

Newspapers and magazines often make money by selling advertising space. The advertising department is way behind today — we need to get an ad ready for today's paper.

Your assignment is to create a 3" x 5" advertisement for the Primitive Flush Company. You can either create your own ad or cut out the pictures below and paste them into the square. I look forward to seeing what you come up with.

Your Editor,

World Times

P.S. You can read more about flush toilets on panel 2 of the *Big Book of History*.

Create ← your ad here.

Primitive Flush Company

SAVE 20%   **NEW!**

New Technology   **FREE Installation**

Your Help Is Needed!

Computers and ____ often make many ____
It's advertising that ____

Your assignment is ____
Company. You can ____
can pass them on to ____
with.
Your Editor,
World Times

Primitive Flush Company

SAVE 20% | **NEW!**

New Technology | FREE Installation

NOAH'S ARK:
THINKING OUTSIDE THE BOX

Section Two — The Ark

1. Read pages 16–17 in *Noah's Ark: Thinking Outside the Box.*

2. In the last section, we talked about the Bible being the Word of God and the directive God gave to Noah to build the ark. Before we go any further we should define an ark. An ark is a simple boat or ship that provides protection and safety. Draw a picture of what you think the ark looked like.

3. Copy the Scripture found on page 16 below.

_____

_____

_____

_____

_____

_____

_____

_____

_____

Genesis 6:12–15

Section Two — The Ark

WORLD TIMES

LET'S REVIEW

This week we are going to review what we've learned so far in our study of the *Big Book of History*.

First we are going to organize the things we have learned. Then we are going to rearrange the information in an outline format. Finally we will give a simple oral report.

To begin, you will need scissors and glue. You will cut out the squares on this page, then glue them in the squares on the time-line.

Remember, time-lines are one way we can organize information that makes it easier for us to understand the context of that information.

 ·············· *Cut out the squares below* ··················

The Tower of Babel	Flush toilets are invented	The Ice Age
We need a hero! Jesus is our Hero!	God Promises to send a flood to destroy the world	The rainbow is God's sign of His promise
In the beginning, God created the heavens and the earth	God creates Adam and Eve	Man sins and paradise is lost

TIME-LINE SHEET

Paste the squares you cut out into the correct square below.

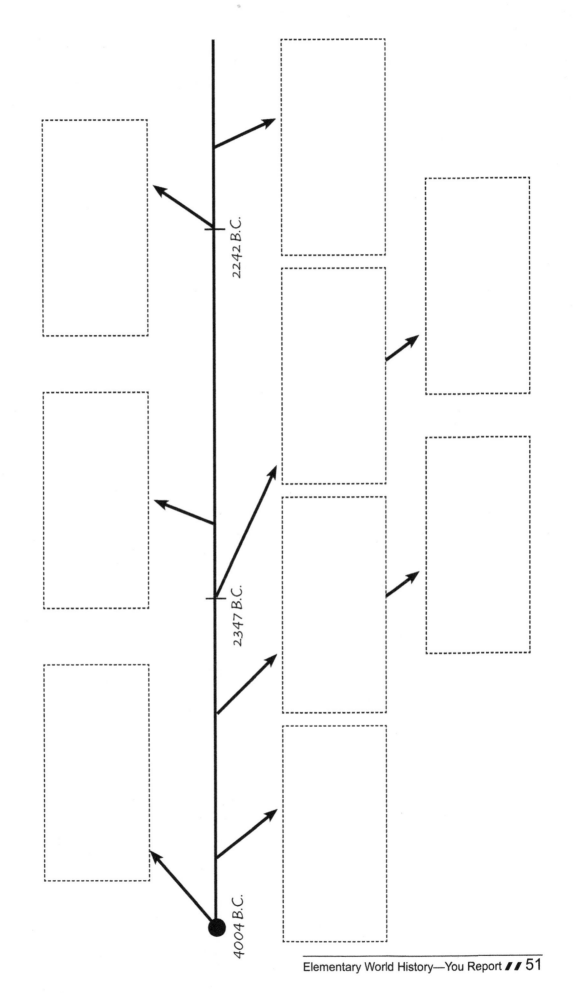

4004 B.C.

2347 B.C.

2242 B.C.

HOW TO WRITE AN OUTLINE

An outline is another way to organize information or important thoughts in a clear, top to bottom or first to last manner. Many students find it helpful to write an outline before writing a report or giving an oral presentation because it gives you a "map" to follow. If your outline is good, your report should be easy to do.

The basic format of an outline is to use an alternating series of numbers and letters, indented accordingly to indicate levels of importance. This is an example of what an outline for what we've learned so far should look like:

The Outline	Instructions
I. In the first section of the *Big Book of History*, I have learned about everything from creation to the invention of flush toilets.	This is where the main idea of your report goes.

II. In the beginning, God created the heaven and the earth.
 	
III. God created Adam and then Eve.
 	
IV. Adam and Eve sin and paradise is lost, and so we need Jesus to save us.
 	
V. God sends a flood to destroy the world.
    A. The rainbow is the sign of God's promise.
    B. The Ice Age is a result of the Flood.
 	
VI. The Tower of Babel is built, and God confuses people's languages.
 	
VII. Flush toilets are invented.
	The body of the report follows the opening statement and breaks down the points you wish to make. Notice some sections have subsections and others do not. You can add as many sections and subsections as you need depending on the information you want to present.

VIII. It is easy at this point to see that God is the Creator of all that we see and that He cares about what happens with His creation.	This is where your conclusion goes.

What We've Learned So Far

I.   In the first section of the *Big Book of History*, I have learned about everything from creation to the invention of flush toilets.

II.   In the beginning, God created the heaven and the earth.

III.   God created Adam and then Eve.

IV.   Adam and Eve sin and paradise is lost, and so we need Jesus to save us.

V.   God sends a flood to destroy the world.

    A. The rainbow is the sign of God's promise.

    B. The Ice Age is a result of the Flood.

VI.   The Tower of Babel is built, and God confuses people's languages.

VII. Flush toilets are invented.

VIII. It is easy at this point to see that God is the Creator of all that we see and that He cares about what happens with His creation.

YOU REPORT!

Using the outline and the information you have learned so far, today you are going to either write a report or give an oral report to your teacher. You can follow the order of your outline. You can also add as many details about what you've learned as you feel your audience would be interested in.

You Report!

FATHER ABRAHAM

God Promises to Bless Abraham

God appears to a man name Abram and commands him to leave his father's house and land and go to the land that He would show him. God also promises to make Abram's descendants into a mighty nation and to bless them.

Through Abram's descendant, all the families of the earth would be blessed. Remember our need for a hero after Adam and Eve sinned? Jesus would be the descendant of Abram who would grant us the blessings of God.

God changed Abram's name, which means "exalted father," to Abraham, which means "father of many."

Copy the following Scripture below.

> **Now the LORD had said unto Abram, Get thee out of thy country, and from thy kindred,**
>
> **and from thy father's house, unto a land that I will show thee:**
>
> **And I will make of thee a great nation, and I will bless thee. . . .**

_____

_____

_____

_____

_____

_____

_____

_____

Genesis 12:1–2

W🌐RLD TIMES

BUILT WITH ROCKS

The Mystery of the Big Rocks

How did they do it? We don't really know. But ancient civilization did it. They built massive structures out of huge rocks.

Look at Panel 3 of our *Big Book of History*. Can you find Stonehenge?

1. How much does the largest stone at Stonehenge weigh?

_____ tons

2. And how many school buses would that be equal to?

_____

Words to Know
Megalithic — Means large stone
Ton — 2000 pounds

Let's Do the Math!

Ask to borrow a calculator from your teacher or parent.

Let's calculate how many pounds the biggest stone at Stonehenge would weigh.

To do this, enter the number of tons (45) times how many pounds are in a ton (2,000). So it would look like this:

$$45 \times 2000 = \text{_____}$$

Now let's figure out how many of you it would take to equal the biggest rock. First we need to know how much you weigh.

Next we take the total number of pounds from our first problem and divide it by how much you weigh.

$$\text{_____} \div \text{_____} = \text{_____} \text{ of you.}$$

This is how many of you it would take to equal the biggest Stonehenge rock.

NOAH'S ARK:
THINKING OUTSIDE THE BOX

Read pages 18 and 19 in *Noah's Ark: Thinking Outside the Box*. In your own words tell how Noah's ark became known as a box.

_____

_____

_____

_____

_____

_____

_____

_____

_____

_____

_____

_____

REMARKABLE STORIES

Often Start with Remarkable Disruptions

Betrayed, nearly murdered, kidnapped, sold into slavery, falsely accused, imprisoned, then promoted to second in charge of all of Egypt. The story of Joseph is a remarkable story.

Find a Bible and look up Genesis 37 to find the answers to these clues and complete the crossword puzzle. Most are from the King James Version.

Across

3. Who was Joseph's father?
5. What did Jacob give to Joseph?
7. What did Joseph get sold as?
8. Who was Joseph sold to?
9. Joseph dreamed a _____.

Down

1. What was Joseph thrown into?
2. Where did Jacob live?
3. Who was sold into slavery?
4. Where did Joseph find his brothers?
6. Twenty pieces of what?
10. What land was Joseph taken to?

WORLD TIMES

GENESIS COMES TO AN END

This is where the Book of Genesis ends and the Book of Exodus begins. So far, we've covered over 2,500 years of history. At this point in history, the children of Jacob (Israel) are living in Egypt as slaves. The world is also becoming a more complex place as powerful empires are rising.

Look at panel 3 of your *Big Book of History* and fill in the dates of each of the following events.

1. The First Assyrian Empire _____ B.C.

2. The Babylonian Empire defeats Assyria _____ B.C.

3. Moses is born in _____ B.C.

4. Write the Ten Commandments as found on panel 3 below.

1. _____

_____

2. _____

_____

3. _____

_____

4. _____

_____

5. _____

_____

6. _____

7. _____

8. _____

9. _____

_____

10. _____

_____

NOAH'S ARK:
THINKING OUTSIDE THE BOX

Flood Legends and Stories

Read pages 20–21 in *Noah's Ark: Thinking Outside the Box*.

Stories resembling Noah's ark are found all over the world, but only the Bible gives us the true account of Noah's ark. We can see from the similarities of the other stories that they came from the biblical account but have mistakes or have lost some of the details over time.

1. One page 21, how many civilizations are there? (across the top)

    _____

2. How many of those civilizations' stories include destruction by

    water? _____

3. How many of those civilizations' stories include a universal destruction? _____

4. How many of those civilizations' stories include an ark provided? _____

5. How many of those civilizations' stories include humans being saved? _____

6. Copy the following Scripture below.

    "All scripture is given by inspiration of God, and is profitable for doctrine, for reproof, for correction, for instruction in righteousness."

    _____

    _____

    _____

    _____

    _____

    _____

    _____

    _____

    _____

2 Timothy 3:16

WORLD TIMES

Frogs, Flies, and Death of Firstborns

God commanded the Israelites to leave Egypt, and He sent Moses to lead them. Just one problem — the pharaoh, or king of Egypt, refused to let them go. So God sent ten plagues to Egypt to prove His power over the alleged Egyptian "gods." As seen in the Bible, a plague is an infliction of something very unpleasant that serves as a punishment.

Find 1491 B.C., the Exodus, on panel 4 of your *Big Book of History*. Write the correct number sequence for each plague below:

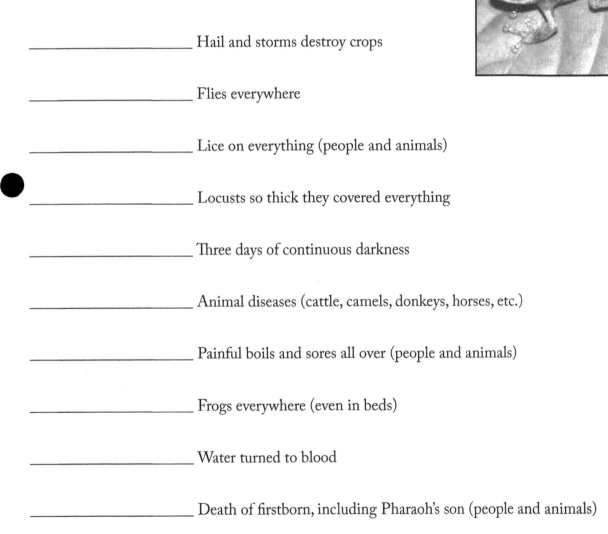

_____ Hail and storms destroy crops

_____ Flies everywhere

_____ Lice on everything (people and animals)

_____ Locusts so thick they covered everything

_____ Three days of continuous darkness

_____ Animal diseases (cattle, camels, donkeys, horses, etc.)

_____ Painful boils and sores all over (people and animals)

_____ Frogs everywhere (even in beds)

_____ Water turned to blood

_____ Death of firstborn, including Pharaoh's son (people and animals)

Frogs, Flies, and Death of Firstborns

LEARNING TO BE GOD'S NATION

Do you remember the man named Abraham and the promise God made to him to make his descendants into a great nation and to give them the land of Canaan?

The children of Israel (who are the descendants of Abraham) have just left the bondage of slavery from Egypt and are headed to Canaan, the Promised Land. But between them and Canaan is the wilderness where the Children of Israel would have to learn to follow God as He makes them into a nation.

In the wilderness, they learn to depend on God for physical provision like food and water. He even gives them a special meal called manna. God also teaches them to depend on Him for protection from their enemies in battle. God does a miracle for them and makes it so their clothing and shoes don't wear out for over 40 years. Wouldn't you like a pair of jeans or sneakers that lasted 40 years?

It is in the wilderness that God gives the Children of Israel the Ten Commandments along with special instructions for how they

are to worship Him. It is here that God gives them the tabernacle, the dwelling place of God's Spirit. Interestingly, God designed the tabernacle to be at the center of their nation in the same way He desires to be at the center of all that we do today.

Unfortunately, the Children of Israel struggled to trust God and to listen to His commands. They also doubted His promise to Abraham that He would give them Canaan. Because of this, most of them did not enter the Promised Land. Instead, they died in their doubt in the wilderness, but the next generation believed God and was able to enter into Canaan and be the nation God called them to be.

Up to this point, God is using a man named Moses to lead them. He now makes Joshua the leader as they cross the Jordan River and conquer their first city in the new land, Jericho. The books of the Bible covering this time period are Exodus (the exit from Egypt), Leviticus, Numbers, Deuteronomy, and Joshua.

At the end of the Book of Joshua, Joshua gives his famous "Choose you this day" speech. On a separate piece of paper, copy the following. Be sure to underline the parts underlined.

[14] **Now therefore fear the LORD, and serve him in sincerity and in truth: and put away the gods which your fathers served on the other side of the flood, and in Egypt; and serve ye the LORD.**

[15] **And if it seem evil unto you to serve the LORD, <u>choose you this day whom ye will serve</u>; whether the gods which your fathers served that were on the other side of the flood, or the gods of the Amorites, in whose land ye dwell: <u>but as for me and my house, we will serve the LORD</u>. — Joshua 24:14–15**

God's Instructions

Here we see that God gave Noah specific instructions in regards to building the ark.

The original language that the Old Testament Scriptures were written in is Hebrew. Over the years, the Bible has been translated into many languages, including English. Sometimes it is difficult to translate from one language to another because there are not words that mean the exact same thing in the new language.

1. Read pages 22–23 in *Noah's Ark: Thinking Outside the Box.*

2. Fill in the blanks below:

"Make yourself an _____ of _____; make

_____ in the ark, and cover it inside and outside with _____."

3. Look at the English word below and the Hebrew word (in parenthesis) next to it and fill in the blank.

"Gopherwood" (*gopher ets*) means _____
This one is easy to remember when telling the story of Noah. You can say, God told Noah to "Go Pher Wood." Do you get it?

"Rooms" (*qen*) means _____

"Pitch" (*kopher*) means _____

WORLD TIMES

THE TROJAN HORSE

Ever been tricked by someone? The city of Troy certainly was during the Trojan War when they thought the Greek army had sailed away in defeat, leaving behind a huge wooden horse. What they didn't know as they wheeled their prize inside the city gates was that there were 30 soldiers and two spies inside the horse. That night as the citizens of Troy slept, the Greek army returned and the soldiers that were inside the horse opened the city gates to let them in.

Even today, people talk about a trojan horse as a way to describe a trick or strategy that secretly lets something destructive into a secure area.

For instance, there are computer viruses called trojan viruses because they are welcomed into a computer through a seemingly safe procedure like opening an email attachment. A person thinks they are opening a safe attachment, but they are secretly letting in a virus that can damage files and the computer.

Draw a picture of what you think the Trojan horse looked like below.

WORLD TIMES

DAVID VS. GOLIATH

A Boy, a Sling, and a Great Big God

Look up the Book of 1st Samuel, chapter 17 in a KJV Bible. Read the chapter then fill in the blanks below.

And there went out a champion out of the camp of the _____, named _____, of Gath, whose height was six cubits and a span [approximately 9 feet, 9 inches tall]. . . .

And the Philistine said, I defy the armies of _____ this day; give me a man,

that we may _____ together. When _____ and all Israel heard those words of the Philistine, they were dismayed, and greatly _____. . . .

David said moreover, the _____ that delivered me out of the paw of the _____, and out of the paw of the _____, He will deliver me out of the _____ of this Philistine. And Saul said to David, go, and the Lord be with thee. . . .

And he took his staff in his hand, and chose him _____ smooth stones out of the brook, and put them in a shepherds bag which he had, even in a scrip; and his _____ was in his hand: and he drew near to the Philistine…

Then said David to the Philistine, Thou comest to me with a sword, and with a spear, and with a shield: but I come to thee in the _____ of the Lord of hosts, the God of the armies of Israel, whom thou has defied. . . .

And all this assembly shall know that the Lord saveth not with sword and spear: for the _____ is the Lord's, and He will give you into our hands. . . .

And David put his hand in his bag, and took thence a _____, and slang it, and smote the Philistine in his forehead, that the stone sunk into his _____; and he fell upon his face to the earth.

So _____ prevailed over the Philistine with a _____ and with a _____, and smote the Philistine, and slew him; but there was no sword in the hand of David.

NOAH'S ARK: THINKING OUTSIDE THE BOX

God's Instructions

1. Read pages 24–25 in *Noah's Ark: Thinking Outside the Box*.

2. Look at the English word below and the Hebrew word (in parenthesis) next to it and fill in the blank.

    "Door" (*pethach*) means _____

    "Cubits" (*ammah*) means _____

    _____

    "Window" (*tshar*) means _____

3. Remember that a cubit is a unit of measure, the distance from your elbow to the tips of your fingers. Even though your "cubit" may be smaller than Noah's cubit would have been, let's measure some things in cubits.

    How many cubits is your bedroom?

    _____ cubits wide by _____ cubits long

    How many cubits long is your bed?

    _____ cubits

    How many cubits is your kitchen table?

    _____ cubits

    How many cubits is your kitchen?

    _____ cubits wide by _____ cubits long

What Is a Cubit?

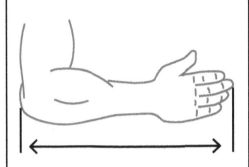

A cubit is measured from the end of the elbow to the end of the fingertips. Because everyone's cubit is different, we have to estimate how long Noah's cubit was. It is estimated that Noah's cubit was about 20 inches long.

WORLD TIMES

DICTIONARIES USED IN CHINA

There is evidence that dictionaries as well as kites were used in China as early as 1000 B.C. A dictionary is a book of words in alphabetical order with information about the word and its meaning.

A dictionary is a great resource for journalists and reporters to look up words and their meanings.

1. Find a dictionary and look up the following words and write their first definition below.

History:

_____

_____

_____

Inspire:

_____

_____

_____

Ancient:

_____

_____

_____

Event:

_____

_____

_____

SOLOMON'S TEMPLE

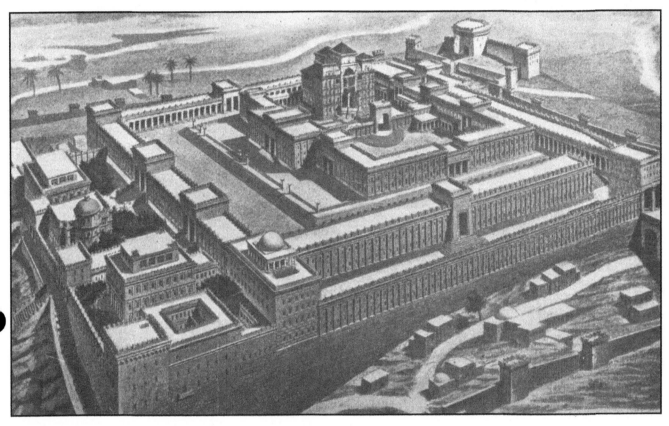

God chose King Solomon, David's son, to build His temple. The temple had much the same design as the tabernacle that was used by the Children of Israel to worship God in the wilderness.

Below is the floor plan of Solomon's temple. Copy the floor plan on a separate sheet of paper.

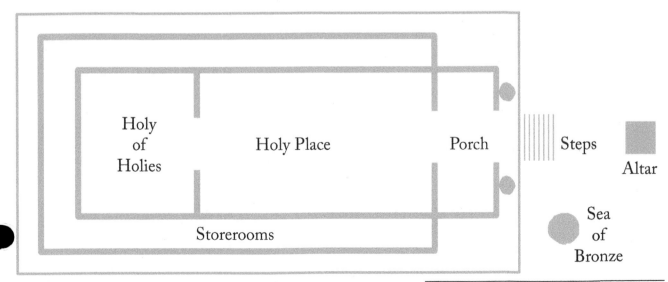

Was the Ark Designed?

1. Read pages 26–27 in *Noah's Ark: Thinking Outside the Box.*

Imagine having to build a ship over 500 feet long, big enough to hold your family and lots of animals along with food and supplies, and strong enough to withstand a global flood. Do you think it would be wise to spend some time making sure you had a good design? I think so. I think Noah probably did as well. I am sure God also helped him with his design and planning.

2. Imagine you're the designer of the ark. How would you design the ark to accomplish everything it had to accomplish? Draw a rough draft of your ark design below or you can use a separate sheet of paper.

LET'S REVIEW

This week we are going to review what we've learned since our last review of the *Big Book of History*.

First we are going to organize the things we have learned. Then we are going to rearrange the information in an outline format. Finally, we will give a simple oral report.

To begin, you will need scissors and glue. You will cut out the squares on this page, then glue them in the squares on the time-line.

Remember, time-lines are one way we can organize information that makes it easier for us to understand the context of that information.

 .... *Cut out the squares below*

> Solomon's Temple

> The Trojan Horse

> David vs. Goliath

> Dictionaries used in China

> Genesis comes to an end

> Frogs, flies, and death of firstborns

> Learning to be God's nation

> Father Abraham

> Built with rocks

> Remarkable stories Joseph

TIME-LINE SHEET

Paste the squares you cut out into the correct square below.

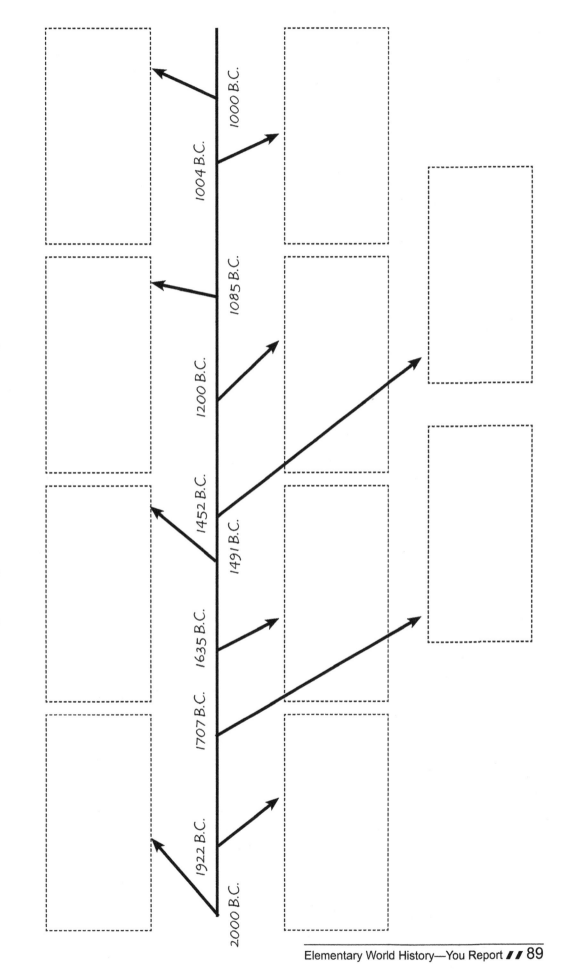

WRITE AN OUTLINE

 Copy the outline below onto a separate sheet of paper

What We've Learned So Far

I.   In the second section of the *Big Book of History*, I have learned about everything from Father Abraham to dictionaries being used in China.

II.   A man named Abraham is given a promise to be a great nation.

III.   Ancient civilizations built megalithic structures.

IV.   Joseph is sold into slavery and becomes second in charge.

V.   The book of Genesis ends, covering 2,500 years of history.

VI.   Frogs, flies, and death of firstborns. The plagues of Egypt.

VII.   The Trojan Horse

VIII.   David versus Goliath

IX.   Dictionaries used in China

X.   Solomon builds a temple for the Lord

XI.   As history continues, we see that God is still involved in His creation and is working with His chosen people to accomplish His will.

W🌐RLD TIMES

YOU REPORT!

Using the outline and the information you have learned so far, today you are going to either write a report or give an oral report to your teacher. You can follow the order of your outline. You can also add as many details about what you've learned as you feel your audience would be interested in.

You Report! 🖊

WORLD TIMES

THE FIRST OLYMPICS

1. From time-line on panel 6 of the *Big Book of History*, fill in the year of the first Olympics above.

2. From the *Big Book of History*, fill in the blanks below.

The Torch

A _____ was kept burning throughout the first _____

games, which began with a single day, and soon lasted for _____ days (three for

events, and two for _____). The fire symbolized the _____

of Prometheus stealing _____ to give to mankind from the Greek gods.

The modern games began in _____, but the torch did not become its

symbol until the _____ games. The _____ is always lit in

_____, Greece — the site of the _____ games.

3. Draw a picture of the torch below.

WⓌRLD TIMES

THE SEVEN WONDERS

Must-See Destinations of the Ancient World

1. Use panel 6 of the *Big Book of History* to write the correct number of the location under the image.

Location Key

1. Mausoleum at Halicarnassus, 351 B.C. — Turkey
2. Colossus of Rhodes; c. 290 B.C. — Greece
3. Great Pyramid at Giza; c. 2580 B.C. — Egypt
4. Temple at Artemis at Ephesus; c. 500 B.C. — Turkey
5. Hanging Gardens of Babylon; c. 600 B.C. — Iraq
6. Statue of Zeus at Olympia; c. 450 B.C. — Greece
7. Lighthouse at Alexandria; 280 B.C. — Egypt

2. Circle the only Ancient Wonder that still exists today.

NOAH'S ARK: THINKING OUTSIDE THE BOX

Figuring Out the Design

"It is the glory of God to conceal a matter;

to search out a matter is the glory of kings."

Proverbs 25:2

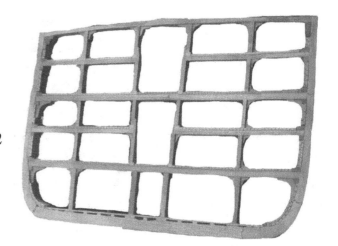

1. Read pages 28–29 in *Noah's Ark: Thinking Outside the Box.*

2. According to the text, what are the three places to look for clues regarding the design of Noah's ark?

   A. _____

   B. _____

   C. _____

3. Complete this paragraph from the book.

   True operational science should not conflict with the Bible. Unfortunately, even . . .

   _____

   _____

   _____

   _____

   _____

   _____

   _____

   _____

WORLD TIMES

DANIEL IN BABYLON

Unfortunately, the Children of Israel forgot to honor God and serve Him. He had promised them when they were still in the wilderness after being delivered from Egypt that they would experience judgment if they failed to worship Him. God kept His promise to them and used Babylon to execute His judgment.

It is in this season of captivity in Babylon where we meet Daniel. The life of Daniel is a great demonstration of the fact that God causes all things to work together for good for those who love Him and are called according to His purposes — Romans 8:28.

Find your Bible and look up Daniel 6 to find the answers to these clues and complete the crossword puzzle. Most are from the King James version.

Across

2. God sent this to shut the lions mouths
3. A King rules his . . . .
5. Darius had been . . . .
6. Daniel was cast into the den of . . . .
8. What was the King's name?

Down

1. Daniel was found . . . .
4. Daniel . . . in his God.
7. Daniel did this three times a day.

WORLD TIMES

DANIEL IN BABYLON

Across

Down

Queen Esther Saves the Israelites

Long before Queen Esther's time, the people of Israel and Judah had been dispersed throughout the land by the Assyrians and the Babylonians. Eventually the Persians conquered nearly all of these empires.

In the Book of Esther in the Bible, we read of a plot by Haman to exterminate all the Jews throughout the Persian Empire, which would have annihilated all of the Jewish people. Esther's daring actions saved the Jewish people from complete destruction, but it also impacts us even today.

Remember Abraham and the promise God made to him to make from him a mighty nation? Do you also remember the

promise to bless all the families of the earth? Well, the Jewish people were the descendants of Abraham. It is from the descendants of Abraham that Jesus, our hero, the One who would bless all the families of the world would be born.

If Esther had not acted bravely and Haman had succeeded, Abraham's descendants would have come to an end and Jesus would not have been born, which means there would be no gospel and no Christian Church. So for those of us who believe in Christ Jesus, Esther's story is also our story.

Copy the following words Esther spoke to her cousin Mordecai when she decided she would go to the king to help save the Jewish people.

. . . and so will I go in unto the king, which is not according to the law: and if I perish, I perish.

— Esther 4:16

_____

_____

_____

_____

_____

_____

Queen Esther Saves the Israelites

NOAH'S ARK:
THINKING OUTSIDE THE BOX

We have finished Section 2 of *Noah's Ark: Thinking Outside the Box*. Copy the following outline of what we've learned on a separate sheet of paper.

I.   In Section 2, I have begun to learn more about Noah's ark through art, legends, and the Bible's instructions for building the ark.

II.   There is artwork depicting what the ark must have looked like.

III.   There are flood legends in many cultures similar to the biblical account of Noah's ark. This would be expected, since they would all be descendants of Noah.

IV.   God gave Noah instructions for building the ark with the dimensions and layout.

V.   It is clear that Noah had a design for the ark.

VI.   In figuring out the design we can look at the following places.

     A. The Bible

     B. Testable science

     C. Traditions and legends

VII.   Even though we don't have exact specifications regarding the ark's design, we can get a rough idea of what the ark would have looked like.

Be sure to save this outline to use with your final project.

W🌐RLD TIMES

ALEXANDER THE GREAT

Greece Becomes a World Power

In 356 B.C., Alexander the Great is born. By the time he dies at age 33, he has conquered most of the known world. Because of this, Greek is the dominant language and will continue to be when the New Testament Scriptures are written. That's why the original language of the New Testament in the Bible is Greek.

It is said that when Alexander the Great came to the sea, he sat down and cried because there was no more for him to conquer.

Looking at the time-line, you can see that Alexander the Great's teacher was Aristotle, who was taught by Plato. Copy the following quotes from each below.

**"I am not afraid of an army of lions led by sheep;
I am afraid of an army of sheep led by a lion." — Alexander the Great**

_____

_____

_____

**"I count him braver who overcomes his desires than
him who conquers his enemies; for the hardest victory is over self." — Aristotle**

_____

_____

_____

"For a man to conquer himself is the first and noblest of all victories." — Plato

_____

_____

_____

WORLD TIMES

Roman Empire Conquers Greece

Empires rise and fall throughout history. So far we have seen Egyptian Empires, the Assyrian Empire, the Babylonian Empire, the Persian Empire, the Greek Empire, and now we see the rise of the Roman Empire. The Roman Empire would be the biggest and most powerful empire to date.

As empires rise and fall, we also see the rise and fall of great leaders. Some are wise, some foolish, some are good, and some are evil. In the Roman Empire, one of the great leaders to emerge was Julius Caesar. But like many great leaders, he made many enemies along the way and was brutally assassinated.

Using panel 8 of the *Big Book of History*, fill in the correct dates for the following events of the Roman Empire.

Julius Caesar

The Roman Empire conquers Greece in _____ B.C.

Julius Caesar defeats Pompey in _____ B.C.

Julius Caesar was assassinated in _____ B.C.

Augustus, the first emperor of Rome, creates an era of peace and wealth in _____ B.C.

Even though it may look like men may make themselves great, the Bible is clear that it is God who establishes them and uses them for His glory and His purposes. On a separate sheet of paper, copy the following two verses.

"Blessed be the name of God for ever and ever: for wisdom and might are his:

And he changeth the times and the seasons: he removeth kings, and setteth up kings. . . ."

Daniel 2:20–21

"The king's heart is in the hand of the LORD, as the rivers of water: he turneth it whithersoever he will."

Proverbs 21:1

Ship-like Proportions

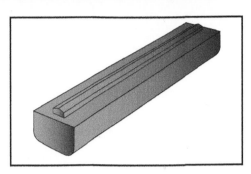

1. Read pages 30–33 in *Noah's Ark: Thinking Outside the Box.*

2. Fill in the blanks below:

"A world class ship _____ center analyzed the biblical ark to see what

would happen if the _____ were modified. By combining measurements of

_____ (capsize resistance), _____ (seakindliness), and

_____ (hull stress), they could not make any substantial _____

on the 4,300-year-old biblical specifications."

3. From the text, the research center concluded the ark could handle waves well over how many feet
    tall?

    _____ feet

4. Copy the definition of "capsize" below.

    Capsize — To overturn, upside down

    _____

    _____

The specifications God gave to Noah for building the ark were perfect for providing stability, comfort, and strength. Some people have a hard time believing the account of Noah's ark and a global flood are true because they only see storybook depictions of the ark. But when we see the actual length, width, and height God told Noah to build the ark, the account becomes much more believable.

WORLD TIMES

THE NEW TESTAMENT BEGINS

Find a Bible to look at as we go through the next section.

As you look at the Bible you are holding, it may look like just one book, but the Bible is actually more like a library of books. The Bible is a collection of 66 books that were written by more than 40 different authors over 1,500 years. The original languages of the books of the Bible were Hebrew, Aramaic, and Greek.

Many books, many authors, many years, many languages . . . but One inspiration. The Bible is the inspired Word of God, and all of the books of the Bible fit together perfectly because God is the ultimate author.

The first 39 books of the Bible are called the "Old Testament." The word "testament" can also mean covenant or agreement. So far, the world history we've

covered occurred during the Old Testament.

We are now beginning to look at history that occurs as part of the 27 New Testament books of the Bible. In the New Testament, we see the promises that God gave to men like Adam and Abraham in the Old Testament now becoming reality.

In the beginning of your Bible, you will find a list of the 27 books in the New Testament. Write them below.

1. _____

2. _____

3. _____

4. _____

5. _____

6. _____

7. _____

8. _____

9. _____

10. _____

11. _____

12. _____

13. _____

14. _____

15. _____

16. _____

17. _____

18. _____

19. _____

20. _____

21. _____

22. _____

23. _____

24. _____

25. _____

26. _____

27. _____

WORLD TIMES

The Difference Between B.C. and A.D.

Looking at panel 9 of the *Big Book of History*, fill in the blanks below.

B.C. is commonly known as "_____ Christ", and A.D. is short for the

_____ phrase for the year of our _____, again linking it to the

birth of _____. A quick thing to remember is that _____ that

occurred in B.C. times was counting _____ from a higher number to a smaller one

— A.D. is the opposite with years counting _____ to a higher number.

Copy the diagram below.

| B.C. = Before Christ | A.D. = Anno Domini (Year of our Lord) |

4004 B.C.   *Counting Down* ⟶   0   *Counting Up* ⟶   2014 A.D.

NOAH'S ARK:
THINKING OUTSIDE THE BOX

Special Report	
Assignment 42	Day 80

Strength

1. Read pages 34–35 in *Noah's Ark: Thinking Outside the Box.*

    When we look at the ark's proportions, the first thing we must determine is how Noah could build an ark 450–500 feet in length that would be strong enough to survive the stress and flex of ocean travel.

2. What were the sea conditions during the Flood? Write the four clues given in the Bible found on page 35.

    1. _____

    _____

    _____

    2. _____

    _____

    _____

    3. _____

    _____

    _____

    4. _____

    _____

    _____

WORLD TIMES

OUR HERO IS BORN!

Remember at the beginning of our story when God promised to send a hero to save us and bless all the families of the world? We have finally reached the point in our story where the hero, Jesus, is born. The birth of the Messiah is one of the most important events in history because it is only through Jesus that our sins can be forgiven and we can be made right with God. That is good news!

For this assignment you will imagine you are "LIVE" on the scene when Jesus is born, and you will be giving a "LIVE News Report" of what is happening. To prepare for the story you will need to read Luke 2:1–20 in your Bible. Then gather up an audience and give them the play-by-play of the events as they occur. You can make notes below to help you remember.

The Birth of Jesus

This is _____ reporting live from Bethlehem!

WORLD TIMES

JESUS IS RISEN!

From the time-line on panel 9 of the *Big Book of History*, fill in the year of the Resurrection of Christ above.

This is a great day in the history of creation. Jesus Christ came to earth, lived a sinless life, became a sacrifice to make payment for the sins of man, was beaten, whipped, and crucified on a cross. But the Scriptures tell us that in three days, He rose from the grave, not only making full payment for our sins but also conquering death itself.

Scripture tells us that if we believe in Jesus and confess our sins (the bad things we have done), that God will forgive us and cleanse us. Where sin separates man from God, Jesus restores the relationship between man and God.

Is Jesus your hero? Have you asked Him to come into your life to make you right with God so you can be forgiven and live forever with Him as His child? If you haven't, then today could be the greatest day in your history, too!

Just pray the prayer below.

Dear God,

I admit that I have done things that I shouldn't have done. I am sorry for doing those things. I know I deserve to be punished, but I believe you sent Your Son, Jesus, to be punished for me. Today, I ask Jesus to be my hero and to come into my life and make me right with You. As Your child, I surrender my life to serve You and bring You glory.

Amen!

If this is the first time you prayed this prayer, let your parent or teacher know.

1. Read pages 36–37 in *Noah's Ark: Thinking Outside the Box*.

   These pages show the modern method of cross-lamination or crisscrossing the planks to add strength as well as the ancient methods of mortise and tenon-jointed planking to help prevent leaking. We can see from these diagrams that the methods did exist to build the ark as God instructed and still be seaworthy.

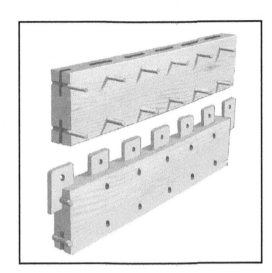

2. Draw the picture at the top of page 37 of the mortise, tenon, dowel, and plank.

LET'S REVIEW

This week we are going to review what we've learned since our last review of the *Big Book of History*.

First we are going to organize the things we have learned. Then we are going to rearrange the information in an outline format. Finally, we will give a simple oral report.

To begin, you will need scissors and glue. You will cut out the squares on this page, then glue them in the squares on the time-line.

Remember, time-lines are one way we can organize information that makes it easier for us to understand the context of that information.

 .... *Cut out the squares below*

Jesus is risen

The New Testament begins

The difference between B.C. and A.D.

Our hero is born!

Queen Esther saves the Israelites

Alexander the Great

Roman Empire conquers Greece

The first Olympics

The Seven Wonders

Daniel in Babylon

TIME-LINE SHEET

Paste the squares you cut out into the correct square below.

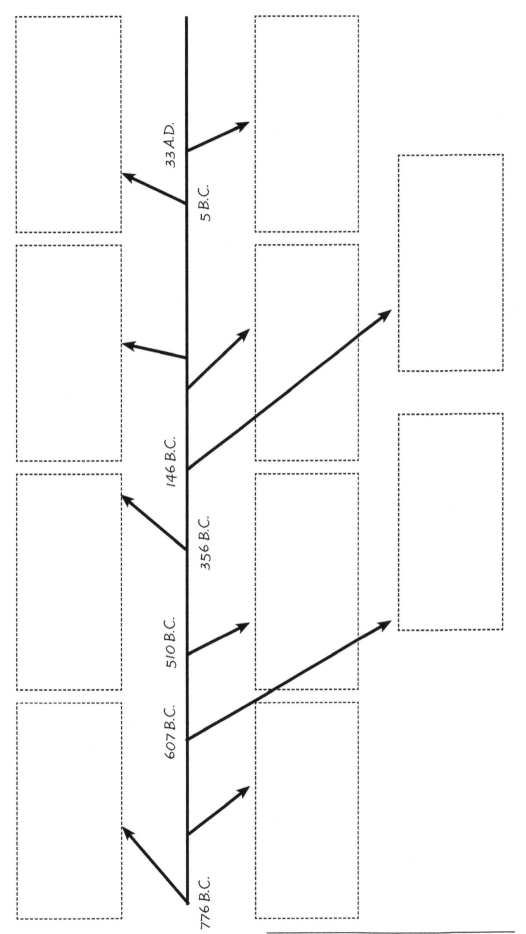

776 B.C.

607 B.C.

510 B.C.

356 B.C.

146 B.C.

33 A.D.

5 B.C.

W🌐RLD TIMES

WRITE AN OUTLINE

 Copy the outline below onto a separate sheet of paper

What We've Learned So Far

I.　In the third section of the *Big Book of History*, I have learned about the events from the first Olympics to the Resurrection of Jesus.

II.　The first Olympics were held in 776 B.C.

III.　Of the Seven Wonders of the Ancient World, only the Great Pyramid remains today.

IV.　Joseph is sold into slavery and becomes second in charge.

V.　Daniel was obedient to God in Babylon.

VI.　Queen Esther saves the Israelites.

VII.　Alexander the Great helps Greece become a world power.

VIII.　After the death of Alexander the Great, Greece is conquered by the Roman Empire.

IX.　The Old Testament ends and the New Testament begins, thus B.C. is known as "Before Christ."

X.　Jesus is born.

XI.　Jesus conquers the grave and I invited Him into my life.

XII.　This is an exciting section because we see the promises of God coming true then as well as today in my life. Jesus is my hero!

WORLD TIMES

YOU REPORT!

Using the outline and the information you have learned so far, today you are going to either write a report or give an oral report to your teacher. You can follow the order of your outline. You can also add as many details about what you've learned as you feel your audience would be interested in.

You Report!

WORLD TIMES

HERO OF ALEXANDRIA

Hero (or Heron) of Alexandria was a Greek mathematician and inventor. He lived in Alexandria, Roman Egypt from A.D. 10–70. He is considered one of the greatest inventors of ancient times. One of his greatest inventions was the first recorded steam engine called the aeolipile. It was also called the "Hero Engine" after its inventor.

There are five inventions Hero of Alexander is credited with on panel 10 of the *Big Book of History*. Write them below.

1. _____

_____

2. _____

_____

3. _____

_____

4. _____

_____

5. _____

_____

W🌐RLD TIMES

COLOSSAL COLOSSEUM

Construction on the Colosseum in the center of the city of Rome, Italy, began in A.D. 70. It was built of concrete and stone and was considered one of the greatest works of Roman architecture and engineering. It is estimated that it could hold 50,000 to 80,000 spectators.

According to the *Big Book of History* on panel 10, when was the Colosseum completed?

_____ A.D.

Words to Know

Amphitheater — an oval or round building with tiers of seats around a central area.

In the box below, sketch a picture of the Colosseum.

NOAH'S ARK:
THINKING OUTSIDE THE BOX

Could Ancient Man Have Built a Boat That Big?

Stories resembling Noah's ark are found all over the world, but only the Bible gives us the true account of Noah's ark. We can see from the similarities of the other stories that they came from the biblical account but have mistakes or have lost some of the details over time.

1. Read pages 38 and 39 in *Noah's Ark: Thinking Outside the Box*.

2. Fill in the blanks below.

Historians were once skeptical of the writings of an ancient _____ historian

that described an oversize catamaran galley, _____. At 420 feet, it

was almost ark-sized, which, in _____ B.C., is way out of order in a presumed

evolution of ships. The description was initially dismissed as pure _____, but

marine _____ kept on dredging up new surprises. As it turns out, ancient

_____ were far more _____ than first thought. Today,

_____ is considered a real _____ and the debate has

shifted to how they maneuvered such a huge _____.

WORLD TIMES

DEATH AS A SPORT

"Public executions, gladiators battling to the death, and killing wild beasts were all ways Roman crowds were entertained. Often if was a challenge to see how brutal it could be. Christians found themselves in the arena facing death and torture because of their faith."

Look at the picture below, then write in your own words what you think is happening.

_____

_____

_____

_____

_____

_____

_____

WORLD TIMES

YOU'RE NOT MY MUMMY

So what exactly is a mummy, you ask? A mummy is the body of a dead person or animal that has been embalmed or preserved for burial. The practice of making a mummy is called mummification.

Look at panel 11 of your *Big Book of History* and fill in the blanks below.

How is a _____ made? Some cultures used

_____ or other _____

to help _____ the body in this way, while it

happened _____ in other cultures because

of _____ and other factors in the area people

lived. When _____, moisture and bacteria

that break down the _____ are absent so the

body doesn't _____ like usual. Mummies are

often associated with ancient _____ where

the oldest _____ have been found. They exist

elsewhere, including _____. Mummies

of Peru are usually bundled up in either _____

and _____ or woven baskets. Some are

_____ as sitting, while others are curled in a

fetal position.

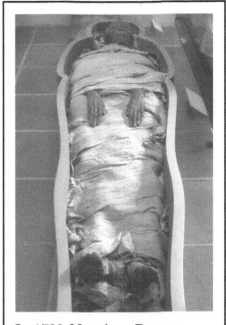

In 1798, Napoleon Bonaparte, a famous French military and political leader would invade Egypt. He took with him scientists and gave them instructions to write down everything they could find about the Egyptians. They recorded things about buildings, statues, religion . . . and mummies. As people around the world read about their findings, they became very curious to learn more about ancient Egypt . . . and thus began the world's fascination with mummies.

NOAH'S ARK:
THINKING OUTSIDE THE BOX

What tools did Noah use?

1. Read pages 40 and 41 in *Noah's Ark: Thinking Outside the Box*.

2. In the box below draw some of the tools you think Noah used to build the ark.

What tools did Noah use?

Brilliant Minds Still Make Mistakes!

Ptolemy

Ptolemy was born in Egypt in A.D. 90 when the Romans were still ruling Egypt. He was known as a mathematician, astronomer, geographer, astrologer, and poet. He is considered one of the most brilliant scholars of his time.

Ptolemy's maps of the known world at that time were amazing and pretty accurate. But not all of Ptolemy's conclusions were right. He believed the earth was fixed, and the sun, the planets, and the stars rotated around the earth. This would later prove false as we would discover the earth rotates around the sun along with the other planets.

Galen

Galen was born in Pergamum in A.D. 131. He was an ancient Greek physician whose views affected the way medicine was practiced for over a thousand years.

Galen's knowledge was partially correct but also flawed. He studied the functions of the circulatory system, nerves, brain, and heart. And while he was right about some things, he was also wrong about others, like "blood letting" which was to cut or allow a leech to suck out a person's blood because they thought this brought healing. This practice proved to be fatal for many people.

What the Bible Says

The Bible says that the wisdom of this world is foolishness with God. Every day men make new discoveries that prove the discoveries of yesterday to be wrong. Only the Creator of everything, God Himself, knows the truth. We always need to trust God over the wisdom of man and science.

On a separate sheet of paper, copy 1 Corinthians 3:18–20.

[18]Let no man deceive himself. If any man among you seemeth to be wise in this world, let him become a fool, that he may be wise.

[19]For the wisdom of this world is foolishness with God. For it is written, He taketh the wise in their own craftiness.

[20]And again, The Lord knoweth the thoughts of the wise, that they are vain.

Brilliant Minds Still Make Mistakes!

What the Bible Says

Chem

Physics

ROMAN EMPIRE SPLIT IN TWO

At this point in history, for over 400 years the huge Roman Empire had dominated the world. Diocletian, a skilled Roman emperor, recognized that the Roman Empire was too big to be controlled by just one man, so he divided the Roman Empire into two halves, Eastern Rome and Western Rome.

Diocletian worked out a system where there would always be two emperors and an assistant for each. This system is called the tetrarchy, which means the rule of four.

Persecution of Christians

Diocletian didn't like the fact that there were many different religions in the Roman Empire, so he forced everyone to worship his gods. In A.D. 303, he began persecuting the Christians. Many Christians moved from Eastern Rome to Western Rome where there was less persecution.

Using panel 12 of *Big Book of History*, fill in the blanks below.

A.D. 293–313 — The four _____ represent the four

_____ of the divided Roman Empire. Each _____

of the empire, _____ and _____, had an

_____ and _____ emperor who co-ruled.

WORLD TIMES

ROMAN EMPIRE SPLIT IN TWO

NOAH'S ARK:
THINKING OUTSIDE THE BOX

Wind, Waves and Broaching

1. Read pages 42–43 in *Noah's Ark: Thinking Outside the Box*

2. Sketch the picture of the big wave below.

WORLD TIMES

THE EDICT OF MILAN

Constantine grew up in the court of Diocletian where he received an excellent education. It was there that he also witnessed Diocletian's persecution and murder of the Christians.

After Constantine became emperor of Western Rome, a civil war broke out and a man named Maxentius declared himself emperor. Constantine and his army marched against Maxentius in A.D. 311.

Constantine's army was about half the size of Maxentius's army. One night before battle, Constantine had a dream where he was told that he would win the battle if he fought under the sign of the Christian cross. The next day they painted crosses on their shields and defeated Maxentius, taking control of Rome.

Constantine believed he was successful because of his conversion to Christianity and because of the support of the Christian God. Because of this, he allowed Christianity to flourish. He formed an alliance with Licinius, the emperor of the east, and they signed the Edict of Milan. This proclamation allowed Christians the freedom to worship, as well as legal rights to build churches throughout the Roman Empire.

Below is a picture of Constantine's symbol, which was a combination of the first two Greek letters of the word Christ. Copy the symbol in the box next to it.

THE EDICT OF MILAN

WORLD TIMES

TRIUMPH OF THE CHURCH

A Turning Point for Early Christianity

The age of Constantine, the Christian emperor, was the turning point for early Christianity. Not only did persecution end in the Roman Empire, but Constantine supported the church financially, built churches, gave favor to church leaders, and promoted Christians to high-ranking positions in the government.

Within the Church, Constantine set out to remove heresy and establish unity. He also had scribes prepare Bibles for the churches.

Through the ages, many ungodly men have tried to destroy the Word of God along with the Church of Jesus Christ. Copy the words of Jesus in regards to His Church below.

"And I say also unto thee, That thou art Peter, and upon this rock I will build my church;

and the gates of hell shall not prevail against it." Matthew 16:18

_____

_____

_____

_____

_____

_____

_____

Thinking Outside the Box

1. Read pages 44–45 in *Noah's Ark: Thinking Outside the Box*.

2. Let's try to build an ark out of paper. If you have a large sink or a bathtub, you can try testing your ark models. Here is a simple one to try.

Take a sheet of paper and fold it loosely in half, lengthwise.

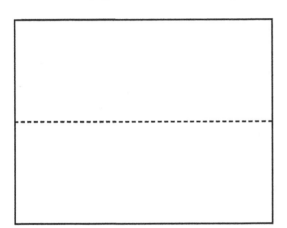

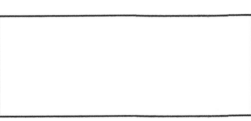

Staple or tape the ends together. Then spread the center out to shape it like a boat.

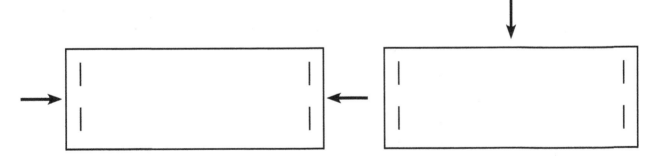

Fill the sink or tub and see if your ark floats. Make some waves and see how your ark responds. Can you make a better design? Go ahead and experiment and see what you can design.

The Bible Is Translated into Latin

This is what John 3:16 looked like in the original Greek:

"Οὕτως γὰρ ἠγάπησεν ὁ Θεὸς τὸν κόσμον, ὥστε τὸν Υἱὸν τὸν μονογενῆ ἔδωκεν, ἵνα πᾶς ὁ πιστεύων εἰς Αὐτὸν μὴ ἀπόληται ἀλλ' ἔχῃ ζωὴν αἰώνιον.

This is what it would have looked like after it was translated into Latin by Jerome. Try reading it out loud:

"Sic enim Deus dilexit mundum, ut Filium suum unigenitum daret: ut omnis qui credit in eum, non pereat, sed habeat vitam æternam."

This is what it looks like translated into English in the King James Bible. Copy this verse below.

Jerome, or Saint Jerome as he is known in the Roman Catholic Church, was commissioned by Pope Damasus I in 382 to translate the Bible into Latin. His translation would be known as the Latin Vulgate.

"For God so loved the world, that he gave his only begotten Son, that whosoever believeth in him should not perish, but have everlasting life."

_____

_____

_____

_____

The Bible Is Translated into Latin

WORLD TIMES

THE BIRTH OF ISLAM

Muhammad was born in A.D. 570 in Mecca, Arabia. When he was about 40 years old, he claimed to have heard messages from the angel Gabriel about God and that he was the appointed messenger to convey these messages to the Arab people. He believed Jesus was appointed to the Jews and that he was appointed to the Arab people. His "messages" make up the Koran, which is the holy book of Islam. The followers of Muhammad are called Muslims.

Read the "did you know?" section on panel 13 in the *Big Book of History*.

Christians then and now believe that Muhammad was a false prophet and that his messages in the Koran were wrong. The writings of Muhammad say Jesus is only a prophet to the Jews, but He was much more than that. He was the Son of God, the one who takes away the sin of the world. True faith acknowledges Jesus is the Son of God and our only source of salvation.

Some people say that we all worship the same God, we just do it in our own way. That is NOT true. Only the living God of creation gets to define how we worship Him and how we receive His salvation. He has revealed to us that it is only through Jesus we can be saved.

Copy the verse below.

"Jesus saith unto him, I am the way, the truth, and the life:

no man cometh unto the Father, but by me." — John 14:6

_____

_____

_____

_____

_____

_____

NOAH'S ARK:
THINKING OUTSIDE THE BOX

Thinking Outside the Box

1. Read pages 46–49 in *Noah's Ark: Thinking Outside the Box.*

2. There are three images on page 49 of items that Noah would have had on the ark. Sketch the three images below.

Lamps

Jars

Oven

LET'S REVIEW

This week we are going to review what we've learned since our last review of the *Big Book of History*.

First we are going to organize the things we have learned. Then we are going to rearrange the information in an outline format. Finally we will give a simple oral report.

To begin, you will need scissors and glue. You will cut out the squares on this page, then glue them in the squares on the time-line.

Remember, time-lines are one way we can organize information that makes it easier for us to understand the context of that information.

 ············· *Cut out the squares below*

> The Birth of Islam
> Muhammad

> The Edict of Milan
> Constantine's rule

> Triumph of the Church

> Jerome translates
> Bible into Latin

> You're not my Mummy

> Ptolomy & Galen
> Brilliantly Mistaken

> Roman Empire divided

> Hero of Alexandria

> Colossal Colosseum

> Death as a sport
> Christian persecution

TIME-LINE SHEET

Paste the squares you cut out into the correct square below.

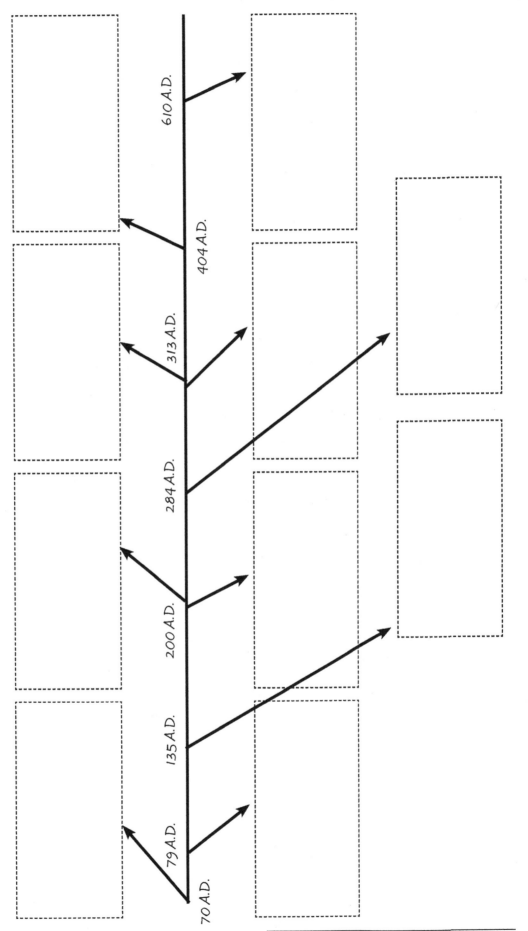

70 A.D.

79 A.D.

135 A.D.

200 A.D.

284 A.D.

313 A.D.

404 A.D.

610 A.D.

WRITE AN OUTLINE

 Copy the outline below onto a separate sheet of paper

What We've Learned So Far

I.   In the fourth section of the *Big Book of History*, I have learned about the events from Hero of Alexander to the birth of Islam covering 540 years of history.

II.   Hero of Alexander was an ancient inventor.

III.   The Colosseum in Rome could hold up to 80,000 people.

IV.   The Roman Empire considered violence and death as entertainment.

V.   Mummification was practiced in many cultures.

VI.   Brilliant minds like Ptolemy and Galen still made mistakes.

VII.   The Roman Empire was divided into Eastern and Western Rome.

VIII.   Constantine's Edict of Milan protected Christians in the Roman Empire.

IX.   The Church flourished with Constantine's support.

X.   Jerome translates the Bible into Latin.

XI.   The birth of Islam through Muhammad.

XII.   As history moves forward, we still see the hand of God directing the affairs of men and accomplishing His purposes through them.

WⒼRLD TIMES

YOU REPORT!

Using the outline and the information you have learned so far, today you are going to either write a report or give an oral report to your teacher. You can follow the order of your outline. You can also add as many details about what you've learned as you feel your audience would be interested in.

You Report! 🖊

GENGHIS KHAN

One of history's most famous warriors is a Mongolian nomad named Genghis Khan, whose name means "Great Ruler." With a fierce but disciplined army, he conquered a huge empire that included substantial portions of central Asia and China. Many of Genghis Kahn's invasions included mass slaughters of the local populations, which earned him a fearsome reputation. So many people were killed in some of the places he invaded that it has taken hundreds of years to rebuild the population. The Mongol Empire would become the largest empire in history.

From the time-line on panel 13 of the *Big Book of History*, fill in the year of Genghis Khan's conquest above.

Copy this famous quote by Genghis Khan below.

"I am the punishment of God. . . . If you had not committed great sins,

God would not have sent a punishment like me upon you." — Genghis Khan

_____

_____

_____

_____

_____

_____

THE BUBONIC PLAGUE

"Lunch with Friends, Dinner in Paradise"

The Bubonic Plague, otherwise known as the Black Death, reached the shores of Italy in the spring of 1348. It is estimated that, by the time the plague was over three years later, up to 50 percent of Europe's population had died.

Signs of the plague were egg-sized swellings in the neck, armpit, and groin areas . . . then black spots appeared on the arms, thighs, or other parts of the body. These spots were a certain sign that the person would die within a day to a week.

Fear caused people to abandon those in need, even children and relatives. The air was filled with the stench of death, and there were so many dead bodies that there were not enough graves for them all. Mass graves holding up to 100 bodies were used to bury the dead.

Black Death was spread initially by fleas on rats and is still found in the world today on some flea-infested rodents.

Person wearing a hat, a mask suggestive of a bird beak, goggles or glasses, and a long gown. The clothing identifies the person as a "plague doctor" and is intended as protection. Descriptions indicate that the gown was made from heavy fabric or leather and was usually waxed. The beak contained pungent substances like herbs or perfumes, thought at the time to purify the air and helpful in relieving the stench. The person also carries a pointer or rod to keep patients at a distance. (Library of Medicine).

Copy the following Scripture on a separate sheet of paper.

[5] Thou shalt not be afraid for the terror by night;

nor for the arrow that flieth by day;

[6] Nor for the pestilence that walketh in darkness;

nor for the destruction that wasteth at noonday.

[7] A thousand shall fall at thy side,

and ten thousand at thy right hand;

but it shall not come nigh thee. — Psalm 91:5–7

Thinking Outside the Box

Read pages 50–51 in *Noah's Ark: Thinking Outside the Box.*
Fill in the blanks below.

HAY: even the big hay eaters like

_____ could be supplemented

with more concentrated _____.

The key to _____ hay is to allow

the animals enough _____ to eat

without _____ all over it. This is

usually done using _____ that allow

the head to go through but not the _____ (and legs). To avoid the manual effort

of _____ hay, it could be dropped from the _____ level into a

_____ on the deck beneath.

For the larger _____, the hay could be stacked solid, with the beasts

_____ their way into the _____ of hay until they were

_____ by _____. These bars then could have been

_____ and the process repeated until they ate their way through the entire

_____.

WORLD TIMES

THE AGE OF DISCOVERY

The Bridge Between the Middle Age and the Modern Age

The Age of Discovery is also known as the Age of Exploration. This is a time when Europeans began exploring the world by sea in search of new goods and trading partners.

It was during this age that explorers were able to learn more about new lands like Africa, the Americas, and China.

This exploration also allowed for global mapping of the world. A new worldview emerged as new civilizations connected with each other.

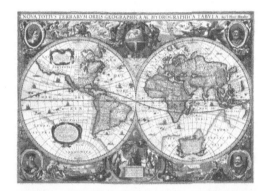

Providential Geography

Geography is the study of the lands, the features, the people and animals, the inhabitants, and the extraordinary aspects of the earth.

History itself belongs to God, the Creator. From the first day to the last, God is causing everything to work together for His purposes and glory. As empires would rise, new trade routes, roads, and paths of communication would also develop. This allowed new people throughout Europe and Asia to hear the Good News of our hero, Jesus Christ.

Kings, queens, and explorers in the Age of Discovery may have thought they were expanding their kingdoms, but what they were actually doing was expanding God's Kingdom. The discovery of new lands and civilizations would also take the message of our hero, Jesus, and the hope of salvation to the ends of the earth. Jesus said this to His disciples as recorded in Matthew 24:14:

"And this gospel of the kingdom shall be preached in all the world for a witness unto all nations; and then shall the end come."

Words to Know

Geography — the study of the lands, the features, the people and animals, the inhabitants, and the extraordinary aspects of the earth.

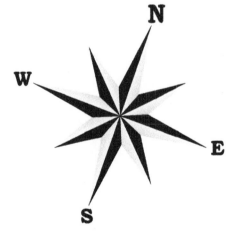

On a separate sheet of paper, draw a map of your yard or neighborhood. Draw as many details as you can. When you are finished, add a compass to show which direction is north, south, east, and west.

The Protestant Reformation

The Protestant Reformation began during the Renaissance. This was a time when more people became educated and learned to read. The Bible was being distributed in languages people could read for themselves rather than having to depend on someone to read it for them and then translate the meaning. As people read the Scriptures, they realized where the Church had gone wrong and where reformation of the Church and its practices were needed.

From panel 14 of the *Big Book of History*, fill in the blanks.

Why So Many?

Have you ever wondered why there are so many different kinds

of _____? It goes back to an important

time in history called the Protestant _____.

It began in _____ and until

_____, across Europe there was a

violent struggle for religious _____

from the Catholic Church. Leaders of the Reformation

_____ preached about the

_____ and salvation in ways that didn't fit

the doctrine of the Catholic Church, which had dominated

Christianity for centuries. Many were publicly tried and

_____ for their defiance, but it didn't stop

the rise of _____.

People and events of the Reformation

John Knox born in Scotland

_____ A.D.

John Calvin born in France

_____ A.D.

Martin Luther in Germany

_____ A.D.

Tyndale burned at the stake

_____ A.D.

Geneva Bible

_____ A.D.

Thinking Outside the Box

1. Read pages 52–53 in *Noah's Ark: Thinking Outside the Box*.

2. On page 53, there is a suggested cross-section of the ark showing central animal cages and food stores against the hull sides. Copy the inside of the cross-section below.

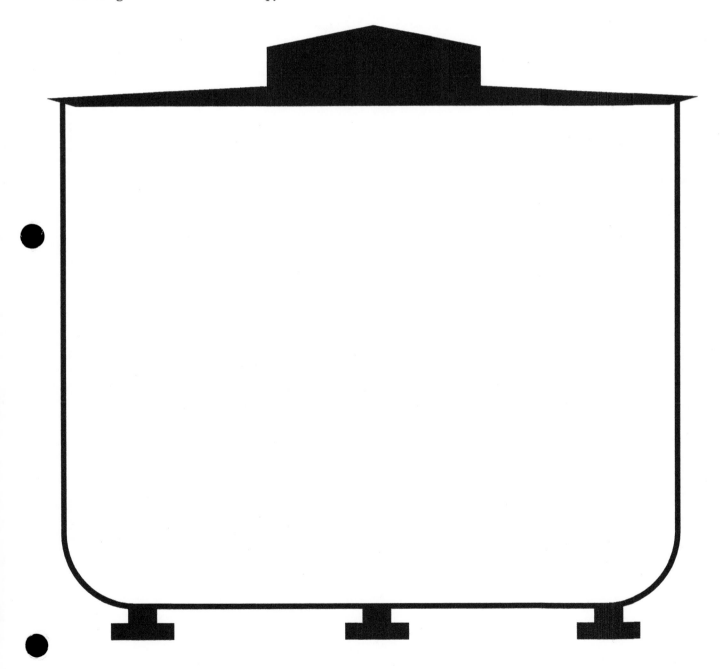

W🌐RLD TIMES

"To Be or Not to Be, That Is the Question"

William Shakespeare, Famous English Playwright

William Shakespeare was born in England in 1564. Today he is considered by many to have been one of the greatest playwrights in history. His plays have been translated into many languages and are still popular. Some of his famous plays include *Romeo and Juliet*, *The Merchant of Venice*, *Julius Caesar*, *Hamlet*, *Macbeth*, and *Othello*.

Words to Know

Comedy — Today it is a play that provokes laughter. In Shakespeare's time it meant a play with a happy ending.

Tragedy — A dramatic play with an unhappy ending.

Below is part of Shakespeare's play *Hamlet* from Act 3, Scene 1. Gather an audience, imagine you are on one of the great performing stages of the world, and read the part of *Hamlet* to them.

Hamlet:

To be, or not to be: that is the question:
Whether 'tis nobler in the mind to suffer
The slings and arrows of outrageous fortune,
Or to take arms against a sea of troubles,
And by opposing end them? To die: to sleep;
No more; and by a sleep to say we end
The heart-ache and the thousand natural shocks
That flesh is heir to, 'tis a consummation
Devoutly to be wish'd. To die, to sleep;
To sleep: perchance to dream: ay, there's the rub;
For in that sleep of death what dreams may come
When we have shuffled off this mortal coil,

Must give us pause: there's the respect
That makes calamity of so long life;
For who would bear the whips and scorns of time,
The oppressor's wrong, the proud man's contumely,
The pangs of despised love, the law's delay,
The insolence of office and the spurns
That patient merit of the unworthy takes,
When he himself might his quietus make
With a bare bodkin? who would fardels bear,
To grunt and sweat under a weary life,
But that the dread of something after death. . . .

"To Be or Not to Be, That Is the Question"

William Shakespeare, Famous English Playwright

W🌐RLD TIMES

PILGRIMS REACH SHORE IN AMERICA

In November A.D. 1620, after three months at sea in a small wooden ship called the Mayflower, 102 pilgrims arrived in America. The place where they came on shore is now known as Plymouth Rock in Massachusetts. There they would establish the Plymouth Colony. Their first year in their new home was very difficult. By the end of the first winter, nearly half of the settlers had died.

William Bradford

One of the Pilgrim Fathers. He was a leader in the Plymouth Colony and would eventually become governor. As a historian, he wrote *Of Plymouth Plantation.* This work told of the Pilgrims' remarkable story as well as the providence of God in leading and caring for them.

Myles Standish

An English military officer who was hired by the Pilgrims as a military advisor for the new colony. He played a leading role in the defense and leadership of the Plymouth Colony.

Squanto

A Native American who assisted the Pilgrims and became an essential part of their survival in the new land. As a young man, Squanto had been taken as a slave to England where he learned English and learned to be a guide and interpreter. God would later use Squanto's misfortune of being taken as a slave to help save the Pilgrims.

On a separate sheet of paper, copy the following words from the journal of William Bradford shortly after landing in America. This was also soon after his wife had fallen overboard and drowned. (Source: Pilgrim Hall Museum)

"May not and ought not the children of these fathers rightly say: Our fathers were Englishmen

which came over this great ocean, and were ready to perish in this wildernesses;

but they cried unto ye Lord, and he heard their voice, and looked on their adversity."

NOAH'S ARK:
THINKING OUTSIDE THE BOX

Ventilation and Lighting

Read pages 54–55 in *Noah's Ark: Thinking Outside the Box.*

Can you imagine being in the ark with all those animals? It could get pretty stinky after a while if you didn't find a way to get fresh air inside the ark. What are three suggestions you would give to Noah to help him get the old stinky air out and the fresh clean air in?

You can be creative, but remember Noah doesn't have electricity or fuel-powered engines.

1. _____

_____

_____

_____

2. _____

_____

_____

_____

3. _____

_____

_____

_____

_____

The Apple Doesn't Fall Far from the Tree

Born in England in 1642, Isaac Newton is considered by many to be the greatest scientist that ever lived. He was a physicist, mathematician, philosopher, alchemist, and theologian. Among his discoveries, he proved that white light from the sun is actually a mixture of all the colors, invented the reflecting telescope, developed the powerful mathematical tool of calculus, and stated the three laws of motion. His greatest scientific achievement was the formulation of the universal law of gravity.

Newton was also a gifted theologian (someone who studies God). He wrote two books on biblical subjects, *Chronology of Ancient Kingdoms* and *Prophecies of Daniel*. He said, "I find more sure marks of authenticity in the Bible than in any profane history whatsoever."

Isaac Newton's greatest accomplishment in life, over everything, is that this man of gigantic intellect was also a genuine believer in Jesus Christ and in the Bible as God's Word.

Copy Isaac Newton's quote below regarding the need for the universe to have an intelligent and powerful designer.

"This most beautiful system [The Universe] could only proceed

from the dominion of an intelligent and powerful Being." — Isaac Newton

_____

_____

_____

_____

_____

The Apple Doesn't Fall Far from the Tree

FATHER OF SCIENTIFIC METHOD

Galileo, an Italian physicist and astronomer, is known for his discoveries with the telescope and his analysis of the motions of objects on earth. It was Galileo who proved that a bowling ball and a marble would fall to earth at the same rate of speed and hit the earth at the same time.

Perhaps Galileo's most important contribution to science was his approach to experimentation as a way to prove what was thought to be true. Galileo was one of the fathers of what we now call the "scientific method."

The scientific method includes observability, testability, repeatability, and falsifiability.

1. First we observe something in nature, like "things fall."
2. Then we test this theory by dropping things. Do they fall? Do heavier things fall faster?
3. We repeat our test or experiments to see if the result continues to be the same even under different circumstances like different heights, objects, inside versus outdoors, etc.
4. Then we determine if our theory is true or false based on testing. It doesn't become a fact until it can be proven!

Let's Do it

Let's test Galileo's theory of falling objects. Get two objects like a small rock and a big rock and try dropping them from different heights and under different circumstances. Write what you find below:

_____

_____

_____

_____

_____

_____

NOAH'S ARK:
THINKING OUTSIDE THE BOX

We have finished Section 3 of *Noah's Ark: Thinking Outside the Box*. Copy the following outline of what we've learned on a separate sheet of paper.

I.   In Section 3, I have begun to learn more about Noah's ark by looking at the construction of the ark in greater detail.

II.   The proportions of the ark were perfect for surviving the Flood. Studies have shown that the design is perfect and could not have been improved upon.

III.   Using construction techniques like cross-lamination and edge-jointed planking would have given the ark strength to survive ocean-size waves.

IV.   It is possible for ancient man to have built the ark, considering that we see other amazing structures ancient man was able to build.

V.   Life aboard the ark would have been difficult but not impossible. Noah needed to be creative with storage, feeding areas, lighting, and ventilation.

VII.   We don't know the actual design of the ark, but we are able to look at ideas and models that let us know that the ark is feasible based on the proportions, design, and technology available.

Be sure to save this outline to use with your final project.

WORLD TIMES

THE AGE OF REASON

Find the Age of Reason on panel 16 of the *Big Book of History* and fill in the blanks.

Embracing the spirit of _____ or the

search for _____, this would be an age where

the _____ of man were many. Yet, with

new _____ and _____

came a desire to _____ long-held biblical

principals and _____. It marks the time when

efforts to rely on _____ ideas led to a

_____ in biblical authority.

Copy the last few sentences of Jonathon Edwards, "Sinners in the Hands of an Angry God."

> **Therefore, let every one that is out of Christ, now awake
> and flee from the wrath to come. The wrath of Almighty God
> is now undoubtedly hanging over every unregenerate sinner.
> Let every one flee out of Sodom.**

The Great Awakening — A.D. 1730–1760

The Great Awakening was a period of revival that spread through the colonies. Jonathan Edwards is recognized as one of America's most important preachers of that time. He was also a scientist who believed all of creation points to a Creator. His sermon "Sinners in the Hands of an Angry God" is a classic example of the messages he preached.

_____

_____

_____

_____

WORLD TIMES

THE INDUSTRIAL REVOLUTION

1. From the time-line on panel 16 of the *Big Book of History*, fill in the years of the Industrial Revolution above.

2. Find the Industrial Revolution on panel 16 of the *Big Book of History* and fill in the blanks.

With a huge shift from _____ labor to more _____

machine-powered _____, mass production of lower-cost goods was possible.

_____ like the steam engine were at the heart of these changes. This would

eventually impact areas of _____, _____,

steel, _____, finance, _____, and more. The

_____ side of these advances was often the _____ condition of

_____ who lived and worked in _____ conditions.

Was Noah's Flood Global?

1. Read pages 56–59 in *Noah's Ark: Thinking Outside the Box.*

2. You make the call, based on what you have learned so far — do you think the whole world was flooded? Or do you think it was only where Noah lived that was flooded?

    This is an opinion question, but support your opinion with why you believe what you believe.

_____

_____

_____

_____

_____

_____

_____

_____

_____

_____

_____

_____

_____

_____

_____

LET'S REVIEW

This week we are going to review what we've learned since our last review of the *Big Book of History*.

First, we are going to organize the things we have learned. Then we are going to rearrange the information in an outline format. Finally we will give a simple oral report.

To begin, you will need scissors and glue. You will cut out the squares on this page, then glue them in the squares on the time-line.

Remember, time-lines are one way we can organize information that makes it easier for us to understand the context of that information.

 ·············· *Cut out the squares below*

Industrial Revolution

Isaac Newton

Galileo
scientific method

The Age of Reason

Protestant Reformation

William Shakespeare

Pilgrims reach America

Genghis Khan

The Bubonic Plague

Age of Discovery

TIME-LINE SHEET

Paste the squares you cut out into the correct square below.

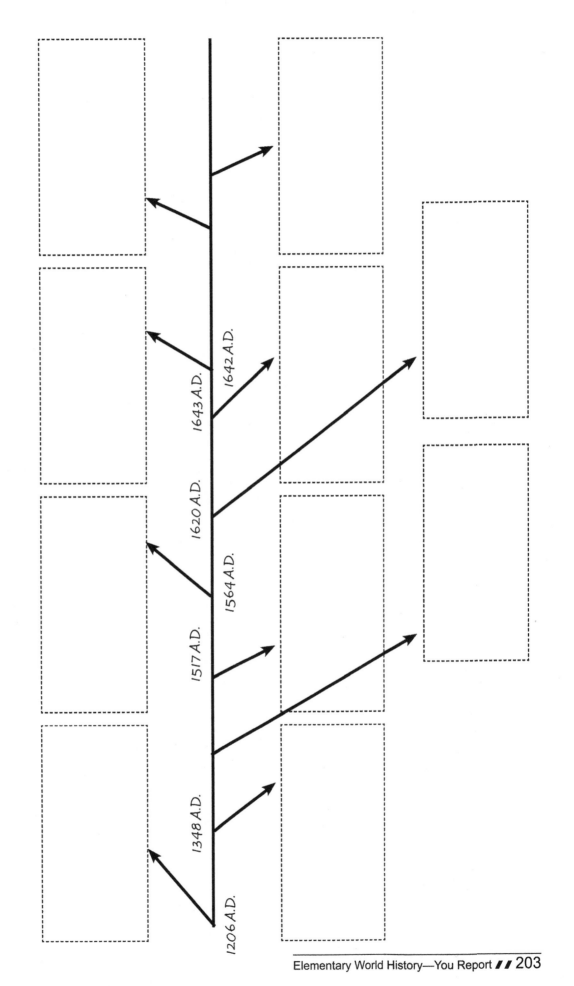

1206 A.D.

1348 A.D.

1517 A.D.

1564 A.D.

1620 A.D.

1643 A.D.

1642 A.D.

WRITE AN OUTLINE

 Copy the outline below onto a separate sheet of paper

What We've Learned So Far

I.   In the fifth section of the *Big Book of History*, I have learned about the events from ruthless barbarians to the Industrial Revolution.

II.   Genghis Khan conquers most of the known world.

III. The Bubonic Plague kills up to 50 percent of Europe's population.

IV.   The Age of Discovery is the bridge between the Middle Age and the Modern Age.

V.   The Protestant Reformation brings change to the church.

VI.   William Shakespeare, "To Be or Not to Be"

VII. The Pilgrims reach shore in America, and the account includes William Bradford, Myles Standish, and Squanto.

VIII. Isaac Newton develops the universal law of gravity.

IX.   Galileo is the father of the scientific method.

X.   The Age of Reason runs from A.D. 1680–1800, and the Great Awakening comes with Jonathon Edwards.

XI.   The Industrial Revolution changes the world's productivity.

XII. We see great discoveries and philosophies in this time period. We see man trying to explain away God, but we also see great revivals. Even in this age, history still belongs to God.

WRITE AN OUTLINE

What We've Learned So Far

WORLD TIMES

YOU REPORT!

Using the outline and the information you have learned so far, today you are going to either write a report or give an oral report to your teacher. You can follow the order of your outline. You can also add as many details about what you've learned as you feel your audience would be interested in.

You Report! 🖊

THE BIRTH OF A NEW NATION

Drafted by Thomas Jefferson and signed by the Continental Congress in 1776, the Declaration of Independence summarizes "self-evident truths" and sets forth a list of grievances against the king. This document symbolized the breaking of ties between the colonies and Great Britain. It contained these famous words:

"We hold these truths to be self-evident,

that all men are created equal,

that they are endowed by their Creator

with certain unalienable Rights,

that among these are Life, Liberty

and the pursuit of Happiness."

George Washington would serve as general and commander-in-chief of the colonial armies in the War for Independence, otherwise known as the Revolutionary War. He would later become the first president of the United States of America.

George Washington is said to have spent an hour each morning on his knees in prayer before a chair on which lay an open Bible.

From the *Big Book of History*, panel 16, fill in the blanks below.

The U.S. Constitution made the _____ of the Declaration of Independence the

_____ of the land, that stated basic human _____ and principles

of _____ government in 1776 A.D.

THE BIRTH OF A NEW NATION

WORLD TIMES

LUDWIG VAN BEETHOVEN

Ludwig van Beethoven, a German composer, is one of the most famous and influential composers of all time. Beethoven was not one of the easiest people to get along with, but he was extremely talented. At the age of 26, Beethoven began to lose his hearing, and he became almost completely deaf at age 44. But even his hearing loss did not prevent him from writing music.

On one occasion, after premiering his 9th symphony, Beethoven had to be turned around after he had finished to see the applause of the audience because he couldn't hear it.

You Be the Critic

To critique something is to review someone's work and make comments on its good and bad qualities. Ask your parent or teacher to help you listen to "Beethoven's 5th Symphony," perhaps from a CD or online. After listening, write your critique or commentary of the music.

_____

_____

_____

_____

_____

_____

_____

_____

_____

NOAH'S ARK: THINKING OUTSIDE THE BOX

Time-line of Noah's Flood

Use pages 60–61 in *Noah's Ark: Thinking Outside the Box* to answer the following questions.

1. How many years after creation was Noah born? _____

2. How many years after creation did God instruct Noah to build the ark? _____

3. How many years after creation was Shem born? _____

4. How many years after creation was Ham born? _____

5. How many years after creation did God instruct Noah to prepare to enter the ark? _____

Noah enters the ark and shuts the door 1656 years after creation. After 100 days, the water starts to recede. In what verse in Genesis 8 is the following found?

6. Tops of the mountains were seen in Genesis 8:_____.

7. Noah sends a raven out of the ark in Genesis 8:_____-_____.

8. Noah sends out a dove for the second time in Genesis 8:_____-_____.

9. The third dove is sent in Genesis 8:_____.

10. Noah removes the covering of the ark in Genesis 8:_____.

11. How many years after creation did Noah and his family leave the ark? _____

WORLD TIMES

FIND THE DATES

From the *Big Book of History*, panel 17, fill in the dates of the inventions from 1800 to 1850 listed below:

1. 1st Steam Locomotive: _____ A.D.

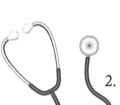

2. Stethoscopes: _____ A.D.

3. Tin Cans: _____ A.D.

4. Braille Printing: _____ A.D.

5. Chocolate Bar: _____ A.D.

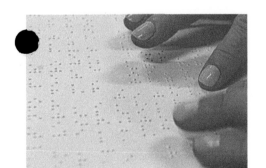

6. Sewing Machine: _____ A.D.

7. Safety Pin: _____ A.D.

WORLD TIMES

Inventors of Fact and Fiction

Thomas Edison was an American inventor who developed many inventions that greatly influenced life around the world. Edison is an example of an inventor whose inventions made the world a better place.

Using the *Big Book of History*, name the nine inventions of Thomas Edison listed on panel 18.

1. _____

2. _____

3. _____

4. _____

5. _____

6. _____

7. _____

8. _____

9. _____

Charles Darwin, an English scientist in the 1800s, is an inventor of a different kind. In 1859, he wrote *On the Origin of Species*, a fictional theory of evolution that would cause many people to lose their faith in God as Creator. Darwin was an inventor of fiction and lies.

Remember our study of Galileo and the scientific method? Darwin's theory of evolution does not use the scientific method because it is not **observable, testable,** or **repeatable.** It is simply a bad conclusion on Darwin's part.

We must remember that God is the author of life and history. Any conclusions we reach apart from that truth are lies.

Inventors of Fact and Fiction

Finding the Ark Today

1. Read pages 62–63 in *Noah's Ark: Thinking Outside the Box*.

2. Fill in the blanks below:

God does not normally preserve _____. The Ten Commandments have been

_____, Solomon's Bronze Sea was _____ up, and the temple

was _____— twice. It seems out of character for _____ to

miraculously preserve Noah's ark.

One thing God does preserve is the _____. It has withstood

_____ for thousands of years. The account of the global Flood is

_____ because the words come from _____ who was

there and knows everything. That should be enough. As we expect, there is plenty of supporting

_____— sedimentary rock all over the _____ pointing to a huge

flood catastrophe, legends of a great _____ found all around the globe, and ample

water in the _____ to cover the earth.

WORLD TIMES

Slavery Ends in the U.S.

Do you remember these words from the Declaration of Independence, written in 1776?

"We hold these truths to be self-evident, that all men are created equal, that they are endowed by their Creator with certain unalienable Rights, that among these are Life, Liberty and the pursuit of Happiness"

By 1861, the United States was divided over the issue of whether or not that included slaves. The northern states (the Union) felt that slavery should end, while the southern states (the Confederacy) felt that slavery was essential to their economy. This became a struggle over the power of the federal government versus the state governments.

The American Civil War began in April 1861 and ended in May 1865. The human cost of the Civil War was greater than anyone could imagine. Over 650,000 Americans died in combat or in captivity, proving to be one of the bloodiest wars in U.S. history.

Below is the famous Gettysburg Address, given by President Abraham Lincoln after what would prove to be one of the worst battles of the war, with over 51,000 dying in battle. He only spoke a few minutes, but his words resound through history. Read the Gettysburg Address out loud to your teacher. Can you memorize it?

Four score and seven years ago our fathers brought forth on this continent a new nation, conceived in liberty, and dedicated to the proposition that all men are created equal.

Now we are engaged in a great civil war, testing whether that nation, or any nation so conceived and so dedicated, can long endure. We are met on a great battlefield of that war. We have come to dedicate a portion of that field, as a final resting place for those who here gave their lives that that nation might live. It is altogether fitting and proper that we should do this.

But, in a larger sense, we can not dedicate, we can not consecrate, we can not hallow this ground. The brave men, living and dead, who struggled here, have consecrated it, far above our poor power to add or detract. The world will little note, nor long remember what we say here, but it can never forget what they did here. It is for us the living, rather, to be dedicated here to the unfinished work which they who fought here have thus far so nobly advanced. It is rather for us to be here dedicated to the great task remaining before us — that from these honored dead we take increased devotion to that cause for which they gave the last full measure of devotion — that we here highly resolve that these dead shall not have died in vain — that this nation, under God, shall have a new birth of freedom — and that government of the people, by the people, for the people, shall not perish from the earth.

Abraham Lincoln
November 19, 1863

Slavery Ends in the U.S.

WORLD TIMES

FIND THE DATES

From the *Big Book of History*, panel 19, fill in the dates of the following from 1900 to 1950:

1. Wright Brothers first powered flight:

   _____ A.D.

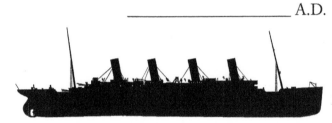

2. Titanic Sinks: _____ A.D.

3. The Scopes Trial _____ A.D.

4. The Holocaust: _____ to _____ A.D.

5. World War I: _____ to _____ A.D.

6. World War II: _____ to _____ A.D.

7. America's first TV Station:

   _____ A.D.

8. Pearl Harbor: _____ A.D.

NOAH'S ARK: THINKING OUTSIDE THE BOX

Ship-Like Proportions

1. Read pages 66–67 in *Noah's Ark: Thinking Outside the Box.*

2. Fill in the blanks below:

A deep _____ of the Grand Canyon exposes an extensive series

of _____ layers. The best _____ is a global-

scale _____ capable of _____ huge amounts

of _____. Each _____ represents variations in

_____ that create different _____ modes.

W🌐RLD TIMES

MAN IN SPACE

Using panel 20 of the *Big Book of History*, write in what happened on the following dates regarding man's exploration of space.

1961 A.D. — _____

1961 A.D. — _____

1969 A.D. — _____

1981 A.D. — _____

1990 A.D. — _____

1998 A.D. — _____

2004 A.D. — _____

2011 A.D. — _____

WORLD TIMES

THE NATION ISRAEL REBORN

May 14, 1948 — The Jews declared independence for Israel as a united and sovereign nation for the first time in 2,900 years. This fulfilled many prophesies and promises of God found in the Bible. Remember when we learned about a man named Abraham and the promise God made to him to make from his descendants into a mighty nation? This is that nation reborn. God is still honoring that promise.

Israel's Law of Return gives Jews the right to come to Israel and live as citizens. Since 1948, Jews from around the world have returned to Israel, the Land of Canaan that God promised to Abraham in 1922 B.C.

Draw the flag of Israel in the box below.

NOAH'S ARK:
THINKING OUTSIDE THE BOX

How Is Christ Like the Ark?

1. Read pages 68–71 in *Noah's Ark: Thinking Outside the Box*.

2. In your own words, explain how Jesus Christ is like the ark.

_____

_____

_____

_____

_____

_____

_____

_____

_____

_____

_____

_____

_____

_____

_____

_____

_____

_____

_____

LET'S REVIEW

This week we are going to review what we've learned since our last review of the *Big Book of History.*

First, we are going to organize the things we have learned. Then we are going to rearrange the information in an outline format. Finally, we will give a simple oral report.

To begin, you will need scissors and glue. You will cut out the squares on this page, then glue them in the squares on the time-line.

Remember, time-lines are one way we can organize information that makes it easier for us to understand the context of that information.

✂ .... *Cut out the squares below* ....

The birth of the U.S.A.	Charles Darwin	Man in space
Ludwig van Beethoven	Abraham Lincoln	Israel becomes a nation
Thomas Edison	George Washington	

TIME-LINE SHEET

Paste the squares you cut out into the correct square below.

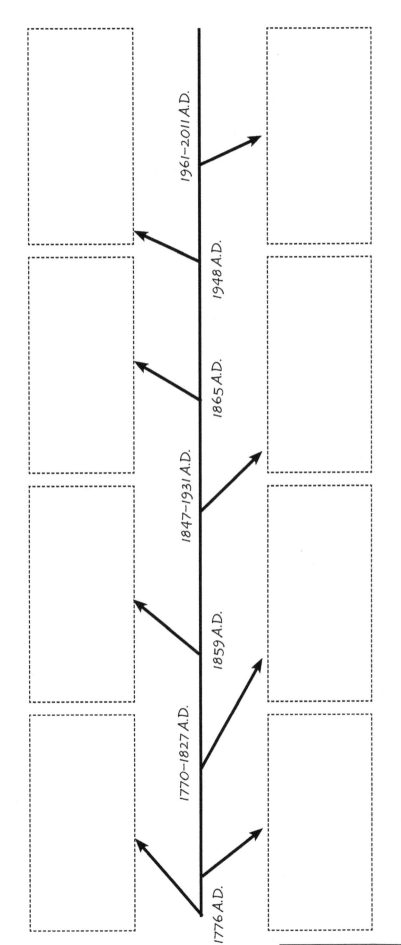

1961–2011 A.D.

1948 A.D.

1865 A.D.

1847–1931 A.D.

1859 A.D.

1770–1827 A.D.

1776 A.D.

WRITE AN OUTLINE

 Copy the outline below onto a separate sheet of paper

What We've Learned So Far

I.   In the sixth section of the *Big Book of History*, I have learned about the events from the birth of the United States of America to man in space.

II.   A nation is born with a Declaration of Independence. George Washington was the commander-in-chief of the Continental Army in the Revolutionary War and would become the first U.S. president.

III.   Ludwig van Beethoven composed amazing music even after he went deaf.

IV.   Charles Darwin created the fictional science of evolution.

V.   Thomas Edison's inventions improved the quality of life, even to this day.

VI.   Abraham Lincoln was president during America's Civil War over the issue of slavery.

VII.   The nation Israel is reborn, fulfilling many biblical prophesies.

VIII.   Man enters space and accomplishes many things.

IX.   There are many great people and events that occurred during this time period of history. Even though it is an age of great advancements, it is evident that men without God are still sinful and capable of great evil.

YOU REPORT!

Using the outline and the information you have learned so far, today you are going to either write a report or give an oral report to your teacher. You can follow the order of your outline. You can also add as many details about what you've learned as you feel your audience would be interested in.

You Report! 🖊

NOAH'S ARK:
THINKING OUTSIDE THE BOX

We have finished Section 4 and 5 of *Noah's Ark: Thinking Outside the Box*. Copy the following outline of what we've learned on a separate sheet of paper.

I.   In Section 4 and 5, I have begun to learn more about the Flood itself by looking at a time-line of the Flood and the evidence we see today.

II.   The time-line of the Flood shows us that Noah and his family spent 376 days in the ark.

III.   Even though we haven't found the ark today, that is not surprising considering God preserves His Word but not usually the icons.

IV.   We see evidence on the earth for Noah's Flood. The Grand Canyon is a prime example of evidence of a global flood.

V.   In the same way Noah and his family were saved from destruction by entering the ark, we as believers in Jesus will be spared from the coming final judgment of God.

Be sure to save this outline to use with your final project.

NOAH'S ARK:
THINKING OUTSIDE THE BOX

It's time to complete your "Pulitzer Prize"–winning special report on *Noah's Ark: Thinking Outside the Box*. Since the beginning of this course, you should have copied four outlines. These outlines will give you the content for your report. When you are finished, your report should fill this page.

Your report will need an opening paragraph (1) that tells the reader what to expect when he or she reads the report, and encourages him or her to read more.

The next portion (2) should be about what you have learned and what you want your audience to learn about as well. Your final paragraph (3) is where you summarize and close your report.

First write the "rough draft" of your report below. When finished, have your teacher review it.

1. _____

_____

_____

2. _____

_____

_____

_____

_____

_____

_____

_____

_____

_____

3. _____

_____

_____

NOAH'S ARK:
THINKING OUTSIDE THE BOX

Once your parent or teacher has reviewed your paper, get the rough draft back with notations for corrections or suggestions to improve your report.

Now, write the final draft of your report below. When finished, give it to your teacher.

1. _____

_____

_____

_____

2. _____

_____

_____

_____

_____

_____

_____

_____

_____

_____

3. _____

_____

_____

_____

WHAT ABOUT YOU?

How Will You Make History?

We have seen that history belongs to God, but oftentimes God chooses to use individuals to make history. As you look at the list on the bottom of the last panel, do you see a way that you would like to make history? Perhaps you are already making history? On the lines below, write how you would like to be a history maker.

_____

_____

_____

_____

_____

_____

_____

Throughout this course we have met many history makers. Who is your favorite? Why?

_____

_____

_____

_____

_____

_____

_____

Answer Keys

Publisher's Note: References to the *Big Book of History* utilize the most up-to-date answers from the 2017 printing.

Assignment 1
Review student's time-line for accuracy.

Assignment 2
Day 1. Heavens, earth, water, light

Day 2. Firmament, sky, waters divided

Day 3. Dry land, plants

Day 4. Sun, moon, stars

Day 5. Flying and sea creatures

Day 6. Land animals and man

Day 7. Rest

Assignment 3
1. Check accuracy of copy work.
2. Word, 40, 1000, Hundreds, resurrection

Assignment 4
man, dust, life, alone, sleep, woman, bone, flesh, Woman, one

Assignment 5
The evidence is the half-eaten apple.

The order is the tree, the serpent, the apple, the flaming sword.

Assignment 6
1. Yes is the correct answer. If no is circled, then additional help is needed from the teacher.
2. Check accuracy of copy work.

Assignment 7
1. Jesus
2. Check accuracy of copy work.

Assignment 8
1. 2347 B.C.
2. 40
3. All
4. 15 cubits
5. 150 days
6. Answers will vary.

Assignment 9
2. God, Scripture, true, mistakes
3. Check accuracy of copy work.

Assignment 10
1. Flood the whole earth
2. A rainbow
3. Make sure rainbow is colored

Assignment 11
Check accuracy of copy work of the "Water then ice" section on panel 2 of the *Big Book of History* time-line.

Assignment 12
Check accuracy of outline copy work.

Assignment 13
1. 2242 B.C.
2. One
3. To heaven
4. Confused the languages
5. Babel
6. Answers will vary.

Assignment 14
Answers will vary.

Assignment 15
2. Drawings will vary.
3. Check accuracy of copy work.

Week 6, Time-line Review

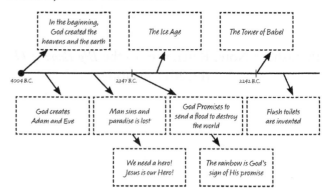

Week 6, Outline Review
Check accuracy of copy work.

Week 6, You Report! Review
Student to do oral or written report.

Assignment 16

Check accuracy of copy work.

Assignment 17

1. 45
2. 4

Let's Do the Math: 45 x 2000 = 90,000.
Remaining answers will vary depending upon the student's weight.

Assignment 18

Answers will vary.

Assignment 19

1. pit
2. Canaan
3. Jacob (across) Joseph (down)
4. Dothan
5. coat (or robe)
6. silver
7. slave
8. Potiphar
9. dream
10. Egypt

Assignment 20

1. 1810 B.C.
2. 1760 B.C.
3. 1571 B.C.
4. The Ten Commandments:
   Don't worship other "gods"
   Don't worship things
   Respect the name of God
   Make time for worship and rest
   Honor your parents
   Don't murder anyone
   Don't cheat on your spouse
   Don't steal
   Don't lie about others
   Don't be jealous of what others have

Assignment 21

1. 20
2. 20
3. 19
4. 18
5. 19
6. Check accuracy of copy work.

Assignment 22

In order

7

4

3

8

9

5

6

2

1

10

Assignment 23

Check accuracy of copy work.

Assignment 24

2. ark, gopherwood, rooms, pitch
3. wood
   nests
   ransom

Assignment 25

Review picture

Assignment 26

Philistines, Goliath, Israel, fight, Saul, afraid, Lord, lion, bear, hand, five, sling, name, battle, stone, forehead, David, sling, stone

Assignment 27

2. Door (or entrance)
   Unit of measure from elbow to tip of fingers
   Midday
3. Answers will vary.

Assignment 28

Answers may vary slightly.

History: a study of past events

Inspire: to influence or encourage somebody to

do something

Ancient: very old, distant past

Event: something that takes place or happens

Assignment 29

Review drawing for accuracy.

Assignment 30

Review drawing

Week 12, Time-line Review

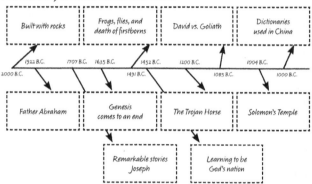

Week 12, Outline Review

Check accuracy of copy work.

Week 12, You Report! Review

Student to do oral or written report.

Assignment 31

1. 776 B.C.

2. fire, Olympic, five, festivals, legend, fire, 1896, 1928, torch, Olympia, original

3. Review drawing

Assignment 32

1. From left to right
    Top: 5, 2, 4
    Middle: 3, 1, 6
    Bottom: 7

2. The Great Pyramid should be circled.

Assignment 33

2. A. The Bible
    B. Testable Science
    C. Tradition

3. …operational science can make mistakes, in which case the Bible overrules. Likewise it would be wise to let operational science

overrule legends.

Assignment 34

1. Blameless

2. Angel

3. Kingdom

4. Trusted

5. Tricked

6. Lions

7. Pray

8. Darius

Assignment 35

Check accuracy of copy work.

Assignment 36

Check accuracy of copy work.

Assignment 37

Check accuracy of copy work.

Assignment 38

146 B.C.

49-45 B.C.

44 B.C.

23 B.C.

Check accuracy of copy work.

Assignment 39

2. research, proportions, stability, comfort, strength, improvement

3. 150 feet

4. Check accuracy of copy work.

Assignment 40

Matthew | Mark | Luke | John | Acts | Romans | 1 Corinthians | 2 Corinthians | Galatians | Ephesians | Philippians | Colossians | 1 Thessalonians | 2 Thessalonians | 1 Timothy | 2 Timothy | Titus | Philemon | Hebrews | James | 1 Peter | 2 Peter | 1 John | 2 John | 3 John | Jude | Revelation

Assignment 41

Before, Latin, Lord, Christ, history, down, up

Check accuracy of copy work.

Assignment 42

1. Logically, a mountain covering, global flood would not be dead calm (Gen 7:19).

2. The ark "moved about the surface of the waters" (Gen 7:18).

3. God "made a wind to pass over the earth" (Gen 8:1). Wind makes waves.

4. The Hebrew word for Flood (mabbul) has a meaning of "being carried along."

Assignment 43

Answers may vary.

Assignment 44

33 A.D.

Follow up with student to see if Jesus is their Hero.

Assignment 45

Review drawing.

Week 18, Time-line Review

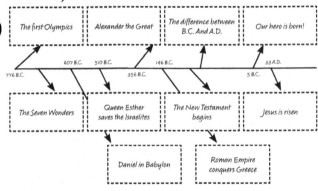

Week 18, Outline Review

Check accuracy of copy work.

Week 18, You Report! Review

Student to do oral or written report.

Assignment 46

1. Aeolipile–the first recorded steam engine

2. Wind-powered organ

3. First vending machine – coin inserted to get holy water

4. Sound effect machines for a theater

5. A version of a syringe

Assignment 47

79 A.D.

Review sketch

Assignment 48

2. Greek, *Tessarakonteres*, 210, exaggeration, archaeology, shipbuilders, capable, *Tessarakonteres*, ship, vessel

Assignment 49

Answers may vary.

Assignment 50

mummy, salt, mixtures, preserve, naturally, weather, buried, body, decay, Egypt, mummies, South America, ropes, blankets, positioned

Assignment 51

Drawings may vary.

Assignment 52

Check accuracy of copy work.

Assignment 53

tetrarchs, emperors, half, Eastern, Western, older, younger

Assignment 54

Review sketch

Assignment 55

Review sketch

Assignment 56

Check accuracy of copy work.

Assignment 57

Check with student to see what was learned from their experiments.

Assignment 58

Check accuracy of copy work.

Assignment 59

Check accuracy of copy work.

Assignment 60

Review sketches

Week 24, Time-line Review

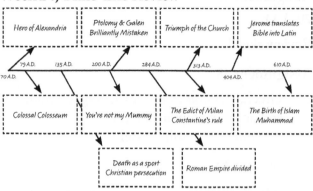

Week 24, Outline Review

Check accuracy of copy work.

Week 24, You Report! Review

Student to do oral or written report.

Assignment 61

1206 A.D

Check accuracy of copy work.

Assignment 62

Check accuracy of copy work.

Assignment 63

cattle, foods, feeding, access, treading, bars, body, lifting, mezzanine, feeder

kinds, eating, wall, stopped, bars, shifted, room

Assignment 64

Review student's map.

Assignment 65

c.1505 A.D.

1509 A.D.

1517 A.D.

1536 A.D.

1560 A.D

churches, Reformation, 1517, 1648, freedom, boldly, Bible, killed, Protestantism

Assignment 66

Check drawing

Assignment 67

Student is to read aloud.

Assignment 68

Check accuracy of copy work.

Assignment 69

Answers will vary.

Assignment 70

Check accuracy of copy work.

Assignment 71

Answers will vary.

Assignment 72

Check accuracy of copy work.

Assignment 73

enlightenment, knowledge, accomplishments, philosophies, discovery, question, authority, man's, downfall

Check accuracy of copy work.

Assignment 74

1760–c.1890s

manual, efficient, factories, Inventions, agriculture, transportation, railroads, mining, dark, miserable, workers, overcrowded

Assignment 75

Answers will vary.

Week 30, Time-line Review

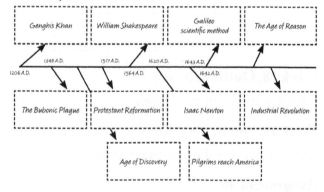

Week 30, Outline Review

Check accuracy of copy work.

Week 30, You Report! Review

Student to do oral or written report.

Assignment 76

principles, law, rights, democratic

Assignment 77

Answers may vary.

Assignment 78

1. 0
2. 1536
3. 1558
4. 1560
5. 1656
6. 5
7. 6–7
8. 10–11
9. 12
10. 13
11. 1657

Assignment 79

1. 1804
2. 1819
3. 1810
4. 1829
5. 1847
6. 1830
7. 1849

Assignment 80

1. Electric voting machine
2. Electric lamp
3. Motion pictures
4. Talking doll
5. Phonograph
6. Recorded music
7. Stock ticker
8. Light bulb
9. Battery electric car

Assignment 81

icons, lost, broken, destroyed, God

Bible, attack, true, One, evidence, earth, flood, oceans

Assignment 82

Student should read speech aloud from paper or from memory if desired.

Assignment 83

1. 1903
2. 1912
3. 1925
4. 1933–1945
5. 1914–1918
6. 1939–1945
7. 1928
8. 1941

Assignment 84

gorge, horizontal, explanation, flood, depositing, sediment, layer, current, sedimentation

Assignment 85

- First man in space is Russian Yuri Gagarin
- First American in space is Alan Shepard
- Moon landing by Apollo astronauts
- First space shuttle Columbia orbited the Earth 37 times
- Hubble Telescope launched onto space
- Construction begins on the International Space Station
- Rovers land and explore surface of mars
- End of the U.S. Space Shuttle Program

Assignment 86

Review drawing

Assignment 87

Answers will vary.

Week 35, Time-line Review

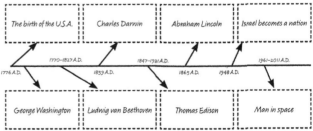

Week 35, Outline Review

Check accuracy of copy work.

Week 35, You Report! Review

Student to do oral or written report.

Assignment 88

Check accuracy of copy work.

Final Assignment – Rough Draft

Make corrections and return to student.

Final Report

Review student's final report

Assignment 89

Answers may vary.

CHARLOTTE MASON INSPIRED
ELEMENTARY CURRICULUM THAT CONNECTS CHILDREN TO
AMERICA'S PAST... AND THEIR FUTURE!

Through this unique educational style, children develop comprehension through oral and written narration, and create memories through notebooking and hands-on crafts. This is not just facts and figures; this is living history for grades 3 through 6.

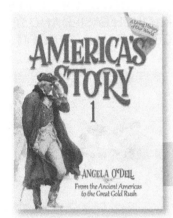

FROM THE ANCIENT AMERICAS TO THE GREAT GOLD RUSH

Part 1: Begins at the infancy of our country and travels through the founding of our great nation, catching glimpses of the men who would become known as the Founding Fathers.

America's Story Vol 1 *Teacher Guide*
978-0-89051-979-0   978-0-89051-980-6

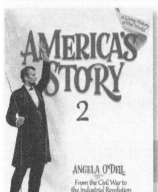

FROM THE CIVIL WAR TO THE INDUSTRIAL REVOLUTION

Part 2: Teaches students about the Civil War, the wild West, and the Industrial Revolution.

America's Story Vol 2 *Teacher Guide*
978-0-89051-981-3   978-0-89051-982-0

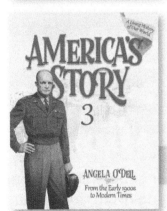

FROM THE EARLY 1900S TO OUR MODERN TIMES

Part 3: Carries the student from the turn of the 20th century through the early 2000s, seeing war through the eyes of the soldiers in journals and letters.

America's Story Vol 3 *Teacher Guide*
978-0-89051-983-7   978-0-89051-984-4